Social Media and Living Well

Social Media and Living Well

Edited by Berrin A. Beasley and Mitchell R. Hancy

LEXINGTON BOOKS
Lanham • Boulder • New York • London

Published by Lexington Books
An imprint of The Rowman & Littlefield Publishing Group, Inc.
4501 Forbes Boulevard, Suite 200, Lanham, Maryland 20706
www.rowman.com

Unit A, Whitacre Mews, 26-34 Stannary Street, London SE11 4AB

British Library Cataloguing in Publication Information Available

Library of Congress Cataloging-in-Publication Data Available

Cloth ISBN 978-0-7391-8927-6
Electronic ISBN 978-0-7391-8928-3
Perfect ISBN 978-1-4985-0886-5

∞ ™ The paper used in this publication meets the minimum requirements of American
National Standard for Information Sciences Permanence of Paper for Printed Library
Materials, ANSI/NISO Z39.48-1992.

Printed in the United States of America

Contents

Introduction

Berrin A. Beasley

What is well-being? Is it a stable income, comfortable home, and time shared with family and friends? Is it clean drinking water and freedom from political oppression? Is it finding Aristotle's "Golden Mean" by living a life of reason and moderation? Scholars have sought to define well-being for centuries, teasing out nuances among Aristotle's writings and posing new theories of their own. With each major technological shift this question of well-being arises with new purpose, spurring scholars to re-examine the challenge of living the good life in light of significantly altered conditions.

Social media comprise the latest technological shift, and in this book leading scholars in the philosophy and communication disciplines bring together their knowledge and expertise in an attempt to define what well-being means in this perpetually connected environment. From its blog prototype in the mid- to late 2000s to its microblogging reality of today, users have been both invigorated and perplexed by social media's seemingly near-instant propagation. Platforms such as Facebook, Twitter, YouTube, Instagram, and LinkedIn have been hailed as everything from revolutionary to personally and societally destructive.

Stephanie Ricker Schulte (2013) wrote that over the past two decades social networks have become a place where life happens "for better or for worse, and a location through which a variety of citizenships and performances of citizenship might emerge" (153). Schulte was referring to the use of social media in a political context, but her point illustrates the idea that social media can affect personal and societal well-being and should be recognized as such.

Support for the effect of social media on well-being can be found in the Egyptian revolution, referred to as part of the Facebook Revolution. In January 2011 Egyptians protested against the country's oppressive leader Hosni Mubarak, calling for his resignation. Facebook was credited with laying the groundwork necessary for the political activism; specifically noted was the Facebook page titled "We Are All Khaled Said," which was created five days after the June 6, 2008, murder of twenty-eight-year-old businessman Khaled Said by Egyptian police. With more than 473,000 users, it became the largest dissident page in Egypt and was the primary location for the planning of the now-famous January 25, 2011, protest (Preston 2011). Facebook page administrators invited participants to the January 25 protest "event" and more than 80,000 clicked yes to attending (Sutter 2011).

Mubarak resigned just eighteen days after the protests began, providing support for the claim that social media use improved the well-being of the protestors and their supporters. "Facebook facilitated an intimate public in that it allowed Egyptians both inside and outside Egypt to connect and feel connected, to participate and feel like they were participating" (Schulte 2013, 157). Of concern to Schulte, and an important observation of the *perception* of social media's power to affect well-being, is that the Facebook Revolution frame "gives more credit to" a "social networking site than to the activists who used it" (Schulte 2013, 162).

Schulte's use of the term "intimate public," first introduced by Lauren Berlant in her book *The Female Complaint*, aptly applies to some aspects of the social media experience and its effect on well-being. Berlant wrote: "An intimate public is an achievement . . . it flourishes as a porous, affective scene of identification among strangers that promises a certain experience of belonging and provides a complex of consolation, confirmation, discipline and discussion about how to live" (2008, viii). Using Berlant's definition of an intimate public to frame the social media experience, it's clear there's more to social media use than simply posting pictures and status updates, acts in and of themselves that could be construed as contributing to an intimate public in relation to one's well-being. It provides "an experience of social belonging in proximity to the technologies that make" it "a site of affective investment and emotional identification" (2008, xi).

In our exploration of the role social media plays in affecting well-being, whether among individuals involved in intimate publics, or society as a whole, this book offers something unique among academic tomes, an introductory chapter by an executive in the social media industry who shares his observations on the ways in which conventions of social communication have changed since the introduction of social media. Ken Gilroy is vice-president of Creative American Greetings International, a division of the greeting card industry's American Greetings Corporation, an international company that earns $2 billion annually. His division focuses solely on internet and social media content and his chapter is intended to bridge the gap between the business perspective and the philosophical perspective of social media, with one acknowledging the necessity of the other. Gilroy's discussion of the evolution of social dialogue to social monologue is filled with implications for a society that has evolved, in his words, from a *me-to-you* conversation to a *me-to-all-of-you-all-about-me* soliloquy. His practitioner's reflection serves as the perfect starting point for an academic exploration of the influence of social media on well-being.

Following his chapter the book is divided into two sections, the first of which concentrates on social media's influence on an *individual's* well-being. The second addresses social media's influence on a *society's* well-being.

Katherine Brittain Richardson begins the first section with her chapter on the application of Aristotle's ideal state of being to social media use. In it Richardson makes the point that a virtuous life, one of moderation and reason, can be difficult to obtain within the overwhelming scope of social media and requires one to cultivate deliberate use of the networks to ensure virtuous pleasure. Teaching youth to moderate their social media use is necessary, she states, to their development of the intellectual and moral values reflective of Aristotle's eudaimonia.

Next, Paul Bloomfield reflects on the nature of friendship and how it's a necessary component of individual happiness. He explores how social media, if not destructive of genuine friendship, promotes a significantly inferior form of friendship in which the distorted image of ourselves we present to our friends online usurps the opportunity for genuine friendship making by hiding our true selves from view.

Joseph Ulatowski discusses whether real-time deception is morally distinguishable from online deception. He argues that because online actions aren't as fine-grained as actions occurring in real time, deceptive characteristics of online personas can be difficult to detect and that failure to do so may lead us to believe the online persona intended to do moral harm.

Pamela A. Zeiser and Berrin A. Beasley engage objective list theory to identify ways in which social media both help and harm an individual's ability to flourish. They use real-life examples of ways in which social media contribute to, and detract from, an individual's physical, emotional, societal, economic, and political well-being. Their chapter highlights specific occurrences, such as cyberbullying and astroturfing, in which social media is at the crux of an individual's well-being.

In part two of the book scholars explore ways in which social media may affect *society's* well-being. Mitchell R. Haney opens with a discussion of memes and how the very structure of social media inhibits, in spite of its potential, rational social discourse about society's most pressing issues. He concludes that the medium motivates a host of fallacious types of reasoning to flourish, inhibiting the types of social discourse necessary for a "community of sanity" constitutive of a flourishing society.

Deni Elliott and Frederick R. Carlson ask whether living life in the social media realm is really living well. Their chapter examines how expectations of privacy change with technology, noting that traditional expectations no longer apply in the social media environment and result in the living of one's life in the public, whether through active consent or coerced consent. Regardless of one's anticipated audience, the permanence of the internet makes possible the later use of words and images shared in social media networks for purposes not intended by the original author.

Alan B. Albarran and Mitchell R. Haney consider the economics of social media by focusing on the ethical challenges of profiting from social media users. Their questions are whether social media companies serve the market (users) or the marketplace (advertisers) or if they can do both. Their analysis is framed in terms of user autonomy and the responsibility of social media companies to protect that autonomy by ensuring users fully understand the user contracts before agreeing to them. Because social media spaces provide the feeling of being in control of one's self-expression and the audiences with whom those expressions are shared, they can lull users into disclosing highly personal information that is then packaged and sold to advertisers, resulting in the kind of tailor-made marketing campaigns traditional forms of media cannot provide.

To complete the volume, Sarah Mattice takes us beyond western borders to contemplate social media from an international perspective. Using China as a case study she considers how the three most prominent religio-philosophical traditions in China, Confucianism, Daoism, and Buddhism, conceptualize well-being and how those concepts are reflected in China's social media network use today.

Because Facebook, Twitter, and a host of other social media networks were created by Americans, many people mistakenly assume Americans are the leading number of users. In reality, China has more than 600 million users, nearly double the number of American users, making Mattice's chapter an appropriate ending to this book. Her work reminds us that much of the philosophical discussion of social media's potential effects reflect an Americanized, westernized perspective, and while a segmented discussion is important to our understanding of the ways in which social media may influence individual and societal well-being, it's only one part of the whole. Intimate publics form around shared interests and experiences, making social media the perfect gathering place for an exchange of information, inspiration, and support, regardless of geographic location. Whether social media enable genuine relationships among intimate public users or provide for their personal, emotional, social, political, and economic well-being are questions the writers of this book seek to answer.

REFERENCES

Berlant, L. (2008). *The Female Complaint: The Unfinished Business of Sentimentality in American Culture*. Durham: Duke University Press.
Preston, J. (2011, February 5). "Movement Began with Outrage and a Facebook Page that Gave it an Outlet." Retrieved July 7, 2014, from nytimes.com/2011/02/06/world/middleeast/06face.html.

Schulte, S. R. (2013). *Cached: Decoding the Internet in Global Popular Culture*. New York: New York University Press.

Sutter, J. D. (2011, February 21). "The Faces of Egypt's 'Revolution 2.0.'" Retrieved July 7, 2014, from http://www.cnn.com/2011/TECH/innovation/02/21/egypt.internet. revolution/.

I

Social Media's Influence on an Individual's Well-Being

ONE

The Social Media Paradox

Ken Gilroy

In the following pages, leading scholars from the philosophy and communication disciplines discuss philosophical considerations and applied ethical issues important to understanding how social media can help us, or keep us from, living a good life. What isn't included in those discussions is a description of the social media experience from a business practitioner's perspective. To meet that need, American Greetings card company executive Ken Gilroy agreed to share his business observations as an introduction to the academic exploration of social media's role in living well.

Gilroy is the vice president of Creative American Greetings Interactive, a division of the American Greetings Corporation, originally a greetings card company that now earns more than \$2 billion annually from printed and online communication goods that manifest around every major event in a person's life, the smaller ones too. He's someone who can contextualize the development of social media to individual and societal well-being in a way that makes it relevant, easily accessible, and that reinforces the pressing need for more research on this topic.

With more than twenty years of experience observing the conventions of social communication, Gilroy explains how the Culture of Us morphed into the Generation of Me, bringing with it a move from the me-to-you communication style of email and instant messaging to the early social media me-to-all-of-you platforms like Friendster and Bebo to the me-to-all-of-you-all-about-me world of Twitter, Facebook, Instagram, YouTube, and the like.

Gilroy's unique perspective regarding this evolution provides the perfect starting point for interdisciplinary academic inquiry into the role social media plays in individual and societal well-being.

—Berrin A. Beasley and Mitchell R. Haney

EMOTIONAL CONNECTIONS

Having a guy from the greeting card industry write a chapter in a book about social media might seem a bit strange. But when you strip away the form factors and think about the shared characteristics between the two—self and social expression content that's used to create emotional connections between individuals though an act of asynchronous conversation—well, maybe the connection between social media and greeting cards isn't such an odd fit after all. Postcards, letters, and greeting cards have served a very human need for social-emotional connection for generations and, like everything else on this planet, those needs have evolved over time.

My job is to lead creative teams in the making and distribution of social expression content, and a big part of my role can be summed up into two simple words: pay attention. I spend a fair amount of time observing the conventions of social conversation and, especially, how those rules and customs evolve and change in ways both big and small. Plain English? I watch how people communicate with each other, and I use those insights to make digital and tangible goods that people will buy.

Since I've been at it for more than twenty years not only have I gotten pretty good at it, but I've also had a front-row seat to witness some really remarkable changes brought about by technological advancement. Over the course of my career I've had the luxury of partnering with some of the best-known names in the tech revolution (Microsoft, AOL) as well as some of the now-forgottens (ICQ, 3 Degrees, Excite). So, more than anything else, this will be a story about change.

TECHNOLOGY'S IMPACT ON COMMUNICATION

The tale of how technology has impact on human communication is a long story indeed—too long, in fact, to cover in any kind of useful way in the time and space allotted. So rather than start with a snooze-inducing story of how better berry pigment selection influenced the durability and social-visual impact of cave drawings, I'm going to hit on some of the key technology highlights from the past fifty or so years to help set the context for what I see happening in the social media space today.

Technological progress, as a label, is a big concept to unpack . . . as well as a tricky thing to put a handle on in terms of describing specifics. So to keep things in a portable format, I've found it useful to think of communication over the last fifty years as being shaped by "Technology Quakes." I tend to look at T-Quakes as groups of game-changing advances that occurred more or less around the same time which, in combination with their after-shocks and evolutions, changed the nature of how most people communicated with one another.

T-Quake 1.0 hit in the 1950s and 60s, and featured the widespread availability of many personal luxuries we barely register as technological advancements today. But it's hard to argue that neighborhood life and community dynamics were forever changed by the enticing new lifestyle of the Great Indoors. The double hammer blows of air conditioning and television made summer evenings spent inside, isolated from neighbors and friends, suddenly a lot more comfortable and entertaining than sitting outside on a hot evening chatting with the neighbors and waiting for things to cool off. The presence of indoor entertainment and comfort began to make neighborhood life a disconnected, solo experience.

When you layer in two more hallmarks of T-Quake 1.0—affordable cars and cheap gasoline—now you're adding community diaspora to the community disconnection. People found themselves able to head out of town for fun and pleasure (get your kicks on Route 66, anyone?) as well as to escape the congestion of city life altogether. With personal transportation within easy economic reach, families could move away from work and public transit hubs and head out to find more space, cleaner air, and new horizons . . . along with all the ready-made housing that sat there waiting. The end result of so many promising T-Quake 1.0 advances was Suburban American Life.

So now that we're all living in the pre-fab oasis, we need something to keep us entertained. It's in that sense I cast T-Quake 2.0 as more of a 1970s/80s phenomenon, and think the era is best represented by the arrival of two key technological totems: personal electronics and cable television.

Music, in its primal sense, remains one of the most social of social medias throughout most of the world—including the United States. Need proof? Just Google image search words like "Bonaroo" or "Warped Tour" and see what comes up. But a curious thing happened in the 70s and 80s. Thanks to cheap electronic imports and ongoing developments in miniaturization, people now had access to audio headphones. Whether on the go (thanks to a Sony Walkman) or in the house (thanks to a parent complaining about "that racket"), music could now become a solo event rather than a broadcast one. You didn't need to share your tastes with those around you if you didn't want to—instead, you could simply pop on your headphones and tune in to tune out.

Other personal electronics—like inexpensive color televisions, first-generation Beta and VHS players, in-dash 8-track and cassette players, and boom box stereos—allowed entertainment to come to you for consumption, rather than requiring you to migrate toward the experience. Unsurprisingly, by the end of the 80s many forms of mass-attendance entertainment—things like movies, the theater, circuses, and even arena-rock-style concerts—were all experiencing ticket sales decline.

Television, on the other hand, retained its stranglehold on the American attention span. For thirty years most Americans had enjoyed—and I mean *really* enjoyed—somewhere between three and five local-market channels on TV. In addition to the steady stream of ads for sugary cereals, one of the primary products pushed by this social medium was cultural glue, with a limited selection of programming providing a cultural bonding experience as well as a built-in conversation starter for most mornings.

Think I'm overemphasizing the social impact of cable television by calling it out? Consider this: When the television series *M*A*S*H* called it quits in 1983, the series finale was viewed by 121.6 million people (60.2 Nielsen rating), and you can bet that it was *the* topic of conversation the next day. More than half of all people living in the United States over the age of *one day old* had tuned in to see Pierce, Honeycutt, and Hotlips Houlihan wave goodbye.

By the end of the decade, however, the splintering cultural effects of having so many more viewing choices available were becoming apparent. Video had killed the radio star on MTV, and niche-targeted broadcasting in general had begun to fracture viewers into smaller groups—this was the incubator age of the 24/7 news and entertainment cycle, and by the end of the decade cable networks like CNN, CNBC, TBS, and TNT were clamoring for—and winning—viewer share. *Roseanne* led the overall pack in the 1989–1990 season Nielsen ratings and yet, even as the number one show, hit a peak rating of only 23.1. Again, the social glue of community was beginning to weaken, and technological advancement was among the root causes.

THE BEGINNING OF THE ONLINE COMMUNICATION PARADIGM

It's time to take a short break from the march of progress and talk instead about the group of people who were born into, and came of age within, this technological test tube. It's time to bring the Boomers to the party.

This massive generational cohort has consciously endeavored to redefine everything it's touched, altering social norms and cultural rites for every milestone they've encountered from adolescence to retirement. This is the generation that wanted to change the world, and they did. But along the way they've also become the bunker-busters of cultural connection, and have brought about a New American Isolation. ✗

They brought it with the McMansion Era, a real estate phenomenon occurring at the intersection of Boomers' earning power and family size. These giant-sized homes ensured that every family member had their own space for personal retreat, plus they were built in rural countrysides without the community infrastructure of traditional cities or suburbs.

They brought it with the Consumerist Economy because, really, why should a family share one iPad when everyone can have their own? Not only have independent media choices continued to increase and fracture audience viewership, but now there are typically more television sets in any given household than residents (U.S. Homes 2010).

They brought it with the Divorced Family, leading the generational pack in divorce rates. Life in two households makes shared social rituals more fleeting and fragile than ever, and further decreases the opportunity for forged connections. Need a wake-up call on this one? Just consider that according to 2012 research by the Hartman Group, 46 percent of all adult meals are now eaten alone, transforming one of the most enduringly social human rituals into a private rite (Eating Alone 2012).

And, finally, they brought it by raising the Indulged Child. They shaved off the sharp edges of life, they liberally applied generous doses of personal technology and self-esteem, and created Gen Y . . . the first crop of American Adolescents. The parental emphasis on the importance of expressing self-identity has de-emphasized the bond-building guardrails of social norms and societal conformity, and the Generation of Me has arrived to usurp the Community of Us.

It is into this environment that T-Quake 3.0 hit the social landscape: the internet, smart phones, and the Culture of Connectivity. The subsequent chapters of this book will explore the depths of this topic, so I'm just going to stick with a couple of facts that have caught my eye as a practitioner in the field . . . namely *how* people are using the technology.

ONLINE TECHNOLOGY USE AND THE ALWAYS-CONNECTED LIFE

Here's a snapshot of where things stand today. The time spent staring at personal media screens in the United States (phones and tablets) now outweighs the time spent watching television, and 66 percent of U.S. tablet owners surf the web while watching TV (Digital Consumer 2014). The fastest-growing segments on social networks are people over fifty-five and 73 percent of the entire U.S. online population has a social networking profile (Cooper 2013; Delo 2013; Social Networking 2014). The Always-Connected Life is on the rise, and the negative outcomes are becoming evident. Giving devices our "complete partial attention" has begun to decrease our ability to focus on tasks, and a recent *New York Times* poll shows that stress levels increase along with the use of mobile devices (Connelly 2010).

But before you take a break from reading to peek at your phone, bear with me as I take you back in time to a simpler age . . . the early 1990s, and the first wave of social media. Because really, that's where the modern concept of uppercase-Social-Media all began.

In retrospect, the 90s-era world of the Internet seems almost impossibly cute and innocent. The early online landscape pretty much consisted of a decentralized group of Internet Service Providers (AOL, Prodigy, CompuServe, et al.) and a user base who was overwhelmingly male and hugely enamored with sending email. The connectivity of the web allowed for "instantaneous" peer-to-peer communication, but the behaviors were purely analogous to offline cultural protocols. One-to-one communication was the norm, and it tended to happen only with people you knew well enough to have physically shaken hands with at some point in your life. Much like writing letters, the online conversational paradigm was asynchronous monologue. . . . I send you something, and then I hear something back—MAYBE—the next time you crank up the modem and dial in to check your inbox. Social communication on the Internet was nothing more than a spare-time hobby, just another form factor—like phone calls, letters, and greeting cards—for folks who were frequent communicators anyway. We were still a society of letter-writers, we had simply figured out how to speed up the delivery.

By the early 2000s the online communication paradigm had begun to shift away from a state of talking with people you already knew, and a new pattern emerged—the Internet became A Place To Meet People. Online communities like AngelFire, Tripod, TheGlobe, and GeoCities began cropping up, giving non-skilled users the first personal publishing tools online and launching the community thread boards that planted the seeds for the current social commenting climate. Chat Client giants roamed the earth, with Web 1.0 success stories like MSN Messenger, AIM, and ICQ getting tens of millions of users among them—and ICQ even offered "Talk with a Random User" features as a foreshadowing of ChatRoulettes to come. Email shook the world when it hit the one-billion-messages-per-day level but, by 2001, AIM alone was handling *ten* billion messages per day among its user base. Online conversational norms began to shift toward real-time dialogue—users hit send, saw that the recipient received the message, and then got a response nearly within the time span of typical verbal conversational realms. At the height of the chat boom, Microsoft launched the Three Degrees product, a chat client with a specific twist: it was set up as a micro-sized peer-to-peer network that allowed users to share content and conversation between a select, invited group of friends. But the dawn of modern social networking had already arrived.

THE RISE OF SOCIAL MEDIA NETWORKS

Social networks had begun to hit the digital landscape like a youthquake in the mid-1990s and by the early 2000s players seemed to emerge out of the woodwork: Friendster, MySpace, Bebo, Hi5, LiveJournal, BlackPlanet,

AsianAvenue, SixDegrees, Classmates, Hub Culture, and more. Friend-ster, launched in 2002, took a cue from the by-then-defunct SixDegrees and aimed to connect only those individuals who shared true real-life common bonds, using an algorithm similar to what's seen in current dating sites. LinkedIn, launched in 2003, took a different path from the youth-focused networks and instead targeted networking professionals. Social network dating sites like OKCupid, Match.com, and Plenty Of Fish arrived on the scene to help connect the romantically inclined. And then, of course, came Facebook—a web property so vast and so well-known as of this writing that I won't even bother discussing it.

The upshot of all this connecting and circling and joining and chatting and tagging and posting and lurking and humble-bragging is that digital social networking changed the online conversational model, perhaps for-ever. Thanks to the rise of the Personal Profile society, talking became a better social strategy than listening, and collecting "Likes" and "Shares" and "Views" became a new social currency, giving everyday people a path to becoming established as thought leaders and/or demonstrating their personal popularity. Conversation shifted away from being a *me-to-you* proposition, and headed toward a more common one-to-many state of *me-to-all-of-you*. And most importantly, it weakened the feedback loop, making a social partner's response a less-than-necessary component of conversation.

Which brings us to the current state of social conversation: it's become a *me-to-all-of-you-all-about-me* world. The arrival of mobile technology into the mix has transformed social media into something we do *while* we're doing something else, and the always-with-me nature of portable com-puting has ensured that no window of free time is too small to fill with a social update. Everyone has suddenly become the curator of their own life, participating in the sort of careful image-crafting which creates a gap between presentation and reality and increases feelings of envy and inad-equacy across all demographic populations. And don't think that the emergence of a "social monologue" conversational paradigm has been lost on the tech industry. Four of the most popular and fastest-growing social media platforms today—Twitter, Vine, Tumblr, and Instagram—aren't modernized walkie-talkies optimized to foster conversation. They're sleek broadcast engines, essentially optimized to function per-fectly well without anyone listening on the other end. More than ever before, social media has led us to dance—alone—along the edge of a solipsistic end game of self-conversation.

And therein lies the social media paradox: the digital tools that were designed with the promise of bringing us closer together have instead led us to a path of greater fragmentation. But where I see promise rising is in context of the larger push toward authenticity that's rolling across the rest of our cultural landscape.

It's easy to spot that return-to-roots philosophy in the restaurant arena with SLO-food (Sustainable, Local, and Organic) dining scenes and farm-to-fork kitchens popping up in towns across America. Likewise, the pursuit of the real and genuine has begun to erode at the McMansion design sensibility. Not only have home sizes begun to drift down to more realistic levels, but new startup architectural design companies like New Avenue Homes are appearing with a novel business model: reinvigorate established neighborhoods by increasing population density. New Avenue provides end-to-end service, helping landowners design, build, permit, and finance amazing small cottages next to the existing dwellings on their lots and, in the process, is working just ahead of the curve to provide affordable and sustainable housing in some of the most desirable neighborhoods around Berkeley and San Francisco. I see it in the greeting card industry as well, with companies like Cardstore, Treat, Minted, and Pear Tree Greetings leveraging the best parts of the digital world (on-demand convenience shopping, cloud-stored photographs, online editing capabilities) to enhance the classic greeting card experience by offering robust personalization and customization options for paper cards that can be mailed—either digitally or physically—with just a few clicks.

THE EMERGENCE OF AUTHENTICITY

But where I'm beginning to see an earnest chase for authenticity to emerge is within the same place where it's currently rare: the social media realm. Small startups are breaking away from the broadcast conversation business model and the one-to-many "monologue enablement" approach, and are beginning to focus the promise of social media, once again, to real connections with the real people in your life. Three such micro-networks belong in any conversation about the next evolutionary path of social networking: Nextdoor, Family Wall, and Couple.

Nextdoor is focused on engaging its members in real-world social contact, and does so within an approach of geographic proximity. A new entrant simply enters his or her physical address at the Nextdoor site, and is admitted to a personalized social network just for their neighborhood . . . and if one doesn't exist yet, a simple step-by-step process lets users create one by mapping out their little corner of the world and becoming the founder of their own neighborhood network. Each private group offers tools and features designed to bring real-world neighbors a little closer together, a sealed digital society with elements of Facebook groups, Craigslist, swap meets, and neighborhood watches stitched together to create an online community. To ensure a true neighborhood focus, each Nextdoor territory is capped at 3,000 households.

Family Wall is probably the most familiar service in a conceptual sense. It's a social network in every commonly understood way, but differentiates itself by being a private network targeted at enriching the "real-world" relationships in your life. Though anyone can create a Family Wall group, the only way to join a circle is to be invited, and unless you're in, you can't access what's being shared. Features of the service are tailored for group sharing; all members can access and edit calendars, photo walls, contacts, and messages. Members in a group can even opt to share their mobile device GPS so others can plot their real-time locations on a map—great for keeping tabs on the kids.

Couple is exactly what the name would suggest: a social network for two, no third wheels allowed. By leveraging the robust sharing tools common to larger social networks and personalizing them to suit a true 1:1 network, Couple lets two people share all of the inside jokes, cute moments, dinner dates, chats, and smiles in one place, and gives them a way to relive those memories simply by scrolling down. True "you & me" features like a shared sketch pad, grocery list, and calendar system leverage technology to bring two people closer together in a very real sense. And in one of its most charming quirks, the app offers two people a way to be together even when apart: the "Thumbkiss" feature. Simply open the app, and press your thumb against the screen—your partner gets the alert to do the same, and you can move your thumbs to the same location on the screen to make a real (and real-time) authentic social connection.

CONCLUSION

A final prognosis? Even in the face of the current state of social media norms, with most conversations being me-to-all-of-you-all-about-me, I remain cautiously optimistic that the social-sharing technology at the heart of the problem can help us arrive at the solution where conversation can once again enrich rather than isolate. That solution itself, however, is more organic than digital in nature—technology can provide us with the most powerful social networking tools and systems we could ever desire but, in the end, it's up to us to resist the narcissistic urge to make it all about ourselves.

REFERENCES

Connelly, M. (2010, June 6). "More Americans Sense a Downside to an Always Plugged-In Existence." Retrieved July 11, 2014, from www.nytimes.com/2010/06/07/technology/07brainpoll.html?_r=0.

Cooper, B. B. (2013, November 18). "10 Surprising Social Media Statistics that will make You Rethink Your Social Strategy. Retrieved July 11, 2014, from www.fastcompany.com/3021749/work-smart/10-surprising-social-media-statistics-that-will-make-you-rethink-your-social-strategy.

Delo, C. (2013, August 1). "U.S. Adults Now Spending More Time on Digital Devices Than Watching TV." Retrieved July 11, 2014, from adage.com/article/digital/americans-spend-time-digital-devices-tv/243414/.

"Eating Alone: The Food Marketer's Hidden Opportunity." (2012, October 18). Retrieved July 11, 2014 from www.hartman-group.com/hartbeat/eating-alone-the-food-marketer-hidden-opportunity.

Smith, A. (2014, February 3). "6 New Facts about Facebook." Retrieved July 11, 2014, from www.pewresearch.org/fact-tank/2014/02/03/6-new-facts-about-facebook/.

Social Networking Fact Sheet. (2014, July 11). Retrieved July 11, 2014, from www.pewinternet.org/fact-sheets/social-networking-fact-sheet/.

"The Digital Consumer." (2014). Retrieved July 11, 2014, from www.slideshare.net/fullscreen/tinhanhvy/the-digital-consumer-report-2014-nielsen/2.

"U.S. Homes Add Even More TV Sets in 2010. (2010, April 28). Retrieved July 11, 2014, from nielsen.com/us/en/insights/news/2010/u-s-homes-add-even-more-tv-sets.

TWO

Eudaimonia or Eudaim[a]nia?

Finding the Golden Mean in Social Media Use

Katherine Brittain Richardson

The lunch menu for today, posted after photos of the dinner entrée from last evening. How many seconds were spent at traffic lights during the morning commute. Selfies. Songs sung (or mis-sung) by a preschooler. Live commentary while watching a TV show or athletic event. Auto accidents videos. In-depth searches for names of people you knew in college, high school, and junior high. Jokes, funny and grim, in good taste and poor. Music mash-ups. Flames and rants. Point/counterpoint critiques of news and editorial posts. Prayers. Six-second dramas. Likes and dislikes. Advertisements. Political rants. Streams of images and text that change continuously, line by line, character by character, one screen to another screen, a cacophony of digital messaging that can inform, amuse, frighten, anger, titillate, and distract users of social media.

Social media have evolved, quickly and dramatically, since the introduction of email, bulletin boards and communities like Friendster, then Myspace, now Facebook, Twitter, Instagram, and Vine. Whether accessed through a personal screen, a mass television screen, or casual conversation, social media content and conventions have become seemingly ubiquitous and normative. Beasley notes, "Social media may have developed from a desire for personal connection, but the result has become a complex account of mediated participation unparalleled by previous communication methods" (Beasley 2013, 2). The evolutionary nature of digital sharing now enabled through the web demands ongoing ethical decision making. Few barriers to participation remain; even the very young participate. "Instant messaging" may be the most true descriptor of our time. Yet plethora alone does not always lead to pleasure.

This chapter will argue that living well with social media requires a commitment to engaging in reflective, thoughtful choices about social media participation so that users may find the pleasure of connectivity, exploration, and expression without the embarrassment, fear, or compulsion that may result from unrestrained screens and screen time. Concomitantly, parents, teachers, and mentors are called to foster the habit of temperate, reflective use among children and teens who live in social-media and Internet-infused cultures through modeling and mentoring so that they, too, may develop the wisdom that will lead to their own "golden mean" of rewarding, wise use.

VIRTUE ETHICS AND THE GOOD LIFE

This chapter does not presume to explain the full extent of Aristotelian ethical theory nor the numerous ways in which virtue ethics have been explored and applied. It seeks to identify several relevant themes that may offer insights into the practicability of ethical habits related to social media use. In such a complex, largely self-regulated, and quickly evolving communication system, an Aristotelian ethical approach seems appropriate for those seeking happiness in daily life without losing perspective or suffering pain. The ethical system argues that the application of practical wisdom, *phronesis*, will reflect the ideal state of being Aristotle called *eudaimonia*, a well-lived life of balance and reason. Ackrill notes, "Eudaimonia is the most desirable sort of life, that life that contains all intrinsically worthwhile activities" (1999, 63). Writing in *The Rhetoric*, Aristotle listed various aspects of virtue: "The forms of Virtue are justice, courage, temperance, magnificence, magnanimity, liberality, gentleness, prudence, wisdom" (*Rhetoric* 1366b1, trans. Roberts). *Phronesis* is demonstrated through behavior that reflects the internal character of such virtue, behavior that demonstrates these across situations and avoids the extremes of vice that would be imprudent or intemperate.

> Virtue, then, is a state of character concerned with choice, lying in a mean, i.e. the mean relative to us, this being determined by a rational principle, and by that principle by which the man of practical wisdom would determine it. Now it is a mean between two vices, that which depends on excess and that which depends on defect; and again it is a mean because the vices respectively fall short of or exceed what is right in both passions and actions, while virtue both finds and chooses that which is intermediate. Hence in respect of its substance and the definition which states its essence virtue is a mean, with regard to what is best and right an extreme. (*NE* II: 6)

Habits are developed as individuals engage in a series of such ethical choices. As Aristotle wrote, "Virtue, then, being of two kinds, intellectual and moral, intellectual virtue in the main owes both its birth and its growth to teaching (for which reason it requires experience and time), while moral virtue comes about as a result of habit" (*NE* II: 1). Such virtuous deliberation trains the mind and character. Burnyeat notes that one must develop an "educated perception" to know how to practice virtues in a given situation (1999, 208). Wiggins explains further, "The [one] of highest practical wisdom is the [one] who brings to bear upon a situation the greatest number of genuinely pertinent concerns and genuinely relevant considerations commensurate with the importance of the deliberative context" (1980, 234). An educated perception helps guide future choices for behaviors; the motivation leads to right action, an inseparable principle of Aristotelian ethics. Thus, the wise life—the good life—is one in which virtue becomes habitual.

SEEKING VIRTUE IN SOCIAL MEDIA USE

A discussion of social media use from a virtue ethics perspective should rightly begin with a discussion of the goodness of the practice. Aristotle taught, "Since activities differ in respect of goodness and badness, and some are worthy to be chosen, others to be avoided, and others neutral, so, too, are the pleasures; for to each activity there is a proper pleasure. . . . As activities are different, then, so are the corresponding pleasures" (*NE* 10: 5). The pleasures and benefits of participation in various social media outlets are identifiable, from individual and organizational viewpoints; from social connectivity to information sharing to political capital to personal amusement, the accessibility and access these media have provided ordinary users are remarkable. The inherent goodness of human communication is not eclipsed by the channel of that communication, so the activity can be justified as one worthy of participation.

But the activity is one that should demonstrate an appropriate balance—a virtuous temperance that avoids the vices Aristotle identified as indulgence and insensibility. In the *Nicomachean Ethics*, Aristotle discussed temperance as a virtue applicable to physical pleasures such as hunger, thirst, and sexuality (see Curzer 1997, 2012). However, this essay will extend the discussion of the virtue beyond the original exposition of Aristotle, asserting that the concept of temperance as the exercise of self-control in the choices of sensual pleasure is applicable to a discussion of living well with any form of media that provides visual, auditory, kinetic, or emotional reward, particularly since the popularization of the touch screen with evocative, involving images delivered through ever improving resolutions challenges users never to be able to look away from the screens or to put them down. The uncontrolled nature of such actions does not demonstrate temperance, but instead the release of unbridled emotions—demonstrating not *eudaimonia* but perhaps something more akin to *eudaim[a]nia*—the type of unreasoned, "incontinent" behaviors Aristotle described as manic: "But now this is just the condition of men under the influence of passions; for outbursts of anger and sexual appetites and some other such passions, it is evident, actually alter our bodily condition, and in some men even produce fits of madness" (*NE* VII: 3).

Just as it was true of the sensual pleasures Aristotle originally considered, excessive or unprincipled use of social media can become a vice: "the self-indulgent man, then, craves for all pleasant things or those that are most pleasant, and is led by his appetite to choose these at the cost of everything else" (*NE* 3: 11). Indeed, some scholars (Kuss and Griffiths 2011; Kim and Haridakis 2009; LaRose, Lin, and Eastin 2003) have noted that heavy use of social media can lead to a form of media dependency, even perhaps some type of media addiction that Block (2008) reported results in increased tolerance for hours of use, withdrawal from other activities, and negative repercussions such as isolation and fatigue. Virtuous actors may want to examine their patterns to determine if they indeed are able to control their use; the "digital stare" of constant on-screen viewing creates a barrier that may prevent users from face-to-face interactions with others in the same time and space. The stereotype of the family at dinner or the couple on a date unable to talk with each other because each is staring at a cell phone screen held in one hand avidly texting and viewing while absentmindedly eating with another may reflect a lack of temperance in the use of social media. Theaters, schools, courts, and churches regularly plead with participants to silence their phones and to put away their screens—and many attendees seemingly find it impossible to sit for one or two minutes without checking for the latest text or photo. The screen fixation has prompted at least forty-four states, the District of Columbia, Guam, Puerto Rico, and the U.S. Virgin Islands to enact laws forbidding texting while driving because of the danger created when drivers are distracted by sending or receiving messages on their phones while also trying to operate a vehicle (Governors Highway Safety Association 2014). More than ten state court systems have developed policies regarding jury use of social media, finding it necessary to admonish jurors not to share or to seek information about the trial and its participants through such platforms (National Center for State Courts).

Perhaps the greatest virtue to be found through social media use is the power of connection with other individuals, and virtues can be demonstrated in many ways through the aesthetic, emotional, and educational outcomes that bring good pleasure through such use. The pleasure and good benefits derived from writing and reading news and opinions, watching and sharing videos and admiring photos, sending snapchats, "friending," and being "friended" are palpable. Indeed, the basis of many social media interactions is friendship, which Aristotle noted "is not only necessary but also noble; for we praise those who love their friends, and it is thought to be a fine thing to have many friends; and again we think it is the same people that are good men and are friends" (*NE* VIII: 1). However, the lack of authenticity in some online relationships can be emotionally damaging and, indeed, demonstrate the vice of insensibility toward others. The pain that comes when one is "unfriended" or the commercial damage that may result from being "unliked" or "flamed" in social media demonstrates the potential outcome with the ephemeral nature of digital relationships. Aristotle noted, "One cannot be a friend to many people in the sense of having friendship of the perfect type with them" (*NE* VIII: 6).

The ease with which Aristotelian virtues such as magnanimity, gentleness, and prudence can be overtaken by the opportunity provided by the pseudonymous or anonymous spheres of social media has led to excesses of snark-filled comments, faked profiles, and group attacks on social media that may damage the value and worth of the human interactions—and may lead to increased risks of depression and suicide (O'Keeffe, Clarke-Pearson, and Council on Communications 2011; Hinduja and Patchin 2010). A 2013 study of Facebook use concluded: "Rather than enhancing well-being, as frequent interactions with supportive 'offline' social networks powerfully do, the current findings demonstrate that interacting with Facebook may predict the opposite result of young adults—it may undermine it" (Kross et al. 2013). Acts of cyberbullying, which the U.S. Department of Health and Human Services defines as "mean text messages or emails, rumors sent by email or posted on social networking sites, and embarrassing pictures, videos, websites, or fake profiles" (stopcyberbullying.org) have reportedly been experienced by some 25 percent of U.S. teens, according to research reported by CNN in April 2013 (Landau). The rise of social media sites that foster "revenge porn" (Hamasaki 2013) or hate speech provide other ready examples of speech acts undertaken without due considerations of risks or harms for self or others—examples of excessive use or insensible actions that reflect more manic meanness than a virtuous mean.

Aristotelian ethics would call for users to examine how their interactions with others are affected when digital communication with others consistently takes precedence over actual face-to-face partnerships with family and friends—and to seek ways in which the goodness of the interactions in both types of arenas can be enhanced through virtuous practices, heeding the Aristotelian principle, "For an activity is intensified by its proper pleasure" (*NE* X: 5).

TRAINING FOR VIRTUOUS USE

How does one develop a desire for and knowledge of virtues? As Aristotle queried, "For this reason also the question is asked, whether happiness is to be acquired by learning or by habituation or some other sort of training, or comes in virtue of some divine providence or again by chance" (*NE* 1: 9). He answered his question by asserting that, "we learn a craft by producing the same product that we must produce when we have learned it, becoming builders, for example, by building and harpists by playing the harp; so also, then, we become just by doing just actions, temperate by doing temperate actions, brave by doing brave actions" (*NE* 1103). Aristotle believed that learning comes through guided practice. If young people are to be equipped to practice *phronesis — displaying the virtues of courage and temperance* as they engage and prepare for the fulfilled life of *eudaimonia* while immersed in the social media-saturated environment — it seems the responsibility for such teaching and modeling must be accepted by parents, teachers, physicians, and other mentors. The explosive growth in technology and the rapidly evolving nature of social communications within and through digital technology make this a daunting task, yet it is a necessary undertaking for those concerned with living well with social media. The undertaking will encompass not only overt teaching strategies but the adoption of virtuous actions by those seeking to serve as models and mentors. Deliberative choice of social media use must be demonstrated to children and adolescents by adults if their teaching is to be taken as valid and virtuous.

Instruction and monitoring of social media community memberships will be important as very young children are now able to engage in viewing, writing, and posting video, print, and graphic content available through the outlets. Media literacy programs that once focused on developing awareness of the commercial and political nature of print and television content should now include instruction in the prosocial and antisocial uses of social media. Monitoring the screen time of children and young people becomes the responsibility of caregivers. This responsibility has been endorsed in a policy statement from the American Academy of Pediatrics (2013), which has advised families to establish a media use plan for their children and for physicians to add two questions addressing access to media and use of media to every child's check-up protocol (Council on Communications and Media 2013). In Korea, concerns about cell phone and Internet addiction have resulted in the development of specific teaching and intervention strategies for use in schools through funding provided by the government to the National Research Foundation of Korea (Koo 2011). Orchestrated campaigns against cyberbullying have been developed in the United States and are being implemented in many school systems.

CONCLUSION

This essay offers no prescription as to an ideal plan for families or schools; the virtuous plan for developing ethical use of social media should be developed through the deliberations of those seeking the best for children and young adults. Cultivating deliberation as a vital aspect of media choice, helping young people understand that there are individuated levels of use that can be found to offer virtuous pleasure without manic excess or excessive deficiencies, is a critical aspect of such teaching. Thus, fostering an awareness of the excesses and deficiencies—*eudaim[a]nia*—that may result from social media and helping younger users adopt habits of virtuous use will promote development of the intellectual and moral virtues Aristotle saw as the fundamentals for lives of *eudaimonia*. As adults commit to modeling, monitoring, and mentoring young people in such virtues, the result should also contribute to increasing the wisdom and pleasure they themselves derive—and through such, all may find better ways to live well with social media.

REFERENCES

Ackrill, J. L. (1999). "Aristotle on *Eudaimonia.*" In *Aristotle's Ethics,* edited by N. Sherman. Lanham, MD: Rowman and Littlefield. 57–77.

American Academy of Pediatrics. (2013). "Media and Children." Retrieved from www.aap.org/en-us/advocacy-and-policy/aap-health-initiatives/pages/media-and-children.aspx.

Aristotle. *Nicomachean Ethics.* Trans. W. D. Ross, in *The Internet Classics Archive* by Daniel C. Stevenson. Retrieved from classics.mit.edu//Aristotle/nicomachaen.html.

———. *The Rhetoric Archives.* Trans. W. Rhys Roberts, in *The Internet Classics Archive* by Daniel C. Stevenson. Retrieved from classics.mit.edu//Aristotle/rhetoric.html.

Beasley, B. (2013). "Introduction" in *Social Media and the Value of Truth,* eds. B. Beasley and M. R. Haney. Lanham, MD: Roman and Littlefield.

Block, J. J. (2008). "Issues for DMS-V: Internet Addiction." *American Journal of Psychiatry* 165: 306–207. DOI:10.1176/appi.ajp.2007.07101556.

Burnyeat, M. F. (1999). "Aristotle on Learning to be Good." In *Aristotle's Ethics,* edited by N. Sherman. Lanham, MD: Rowman and Littlefield. 205–230.

Council on Communications and Media. (2013). "Children, Adolescents, and the Media." *Pediatrics* 2013: 132; 958. DOI: 10.1542/peds.2013-2656.

Curzer, H. J. (1997). "Aristotle's Account of the Virtue of Temperance in *Nicomachean Ethics* III: 10–11." *Journal of the History of Philosophy* 35: 5–25.

———. 2012. *Aristotle and the Virtues.* Oxford: Oxford University Press.

"Cyberbullying." Retrieved from www.stopbullying.gov/cyberbullying/.

Governors Highway Safety Association. (2014). "Distracted Driving Laws." Retrieved from www.ghsa.org/html/stateinfo/laws/cellphone_laws.html.

Hamasaki, S. (2013, December 10). "California Man Charged in 'Revenge Porn' Case." Retrieved from CNN.com from us.cnn.com/2013/12/10/justice/california-revenge-porn-arrest/?iref=obnetwork.

Hinduja, S., and J. W. Patchin. (2010). "Bullying, Cyberbullying and Suicide." *Archives of Suicide Research* 14: 3. DOI: 10.1080/13811118.2010.49413.

Kim, J., and P. M. Haridakis. (2009). "The Role of Internet User Characteristics and Motives in Explaining Three Dimensions of Internet Addiction." *Journal of Computer-Mediated Communication* 14: 988–1015.

Koo, H. (2011). "Development and Effects of a Prevention Program for Cell Phone Addiction in Middle School Students." *Journal of the Korean Academy of Child Health Nursing* 17: 91–99. dx.doi.org/10.4094/jkachn.2011.17.2.91.

Kross, E., Verduyn, P., Demiralp, E., Park, J., Lee, D., Lin, N., et al. (2013). "Facebook Use Predicts Declines in Subjective Well-Being in Young Adults. *PLoS ONE* 8(8): 1–7. DOI: 10.1371/journal.pone.0069841.

Kuss, D. J., and M. D. Griffiths. (2011). "Online Social Networking and Addiction—A Review of the Psychological Literature." *International Journal of Environmental Research and Public Health* 8(9): 3528–3522. DOI: 10.3390/ijerph8093528.

Landau, E. (2013, April 15). "When Bullying goes High-Tech." Retrieved from www.cnn.com/2013/02/27/health/cyberbullying-online-bully-victims/index.html.

LaRose, R., Lin, C. A, and M. S. Eastin. (2003). "Unregulated Internet Usage: Addiction, Habit, or Deficient Self-Regulation?" *Media Psychology* 5: 225–253. DOI: 10.1207/S1532785XMEP0503_01.

National Center for State Courts. "State Links." www.ncsc.org/Topics/Media/Social-Media-and-theCourts/StateLinks.aspx?cat= Judicial%20Ethics%20Advisory%20Opinions%20on%20 Social%20Media.

O'Keeffe, G. S., Clarke-Pearson, K., and Council on Communications. (2011). "The Impact of Social Media on Children, Adolescents, and Families." *Pediatrics* 127: 800. DOI: 10.1542/peds.2011-0054.

Wiggins, D. (1980). "Deliberation and Practical Reason." In *Essays on Aristotle's Ethics*, edited by A. Oksenberg. Berkeley: University of California Press. 221–240.

THREE

Friendship on Facebook

Paul Bloomfield

It seems to be the current zeitgeist that Facebook has been good for friendship: that it has allowed for many new friendships to arise, brought existing friends closer together, allowed them to keep in touch easier, and has been an all-around boon for developing friendships. The thesis at hand is not so much to deny any of these claims in general, but it certainly is to mitigate their significance to the point that we do not see forms of social media per se, such as Facebook, as being genuinely helpful to the *development* of friendship. While there is undeniably a sense of "social" in which any two people interacting are "being social," so that all friendships are in this sense social, the sense of the word at play in "social media" contrasts to the "personal" aspect of friendship which is its "heart and soul," if you will. Perhaps social media isn't generally harmful to nor does it interfere with friendship, but to the degree that it is "social" (contrasting with "personal"), it doesn't promote it either. Crucially, to the degree that it is unresponsive to the different levels of intimacy which can attach to friendships, so that communications are generic or "dumbed down" to the "lowest common denominator" of friendship, accessible to everyone in a wide "circle of friends," this is the degree to which genuine opportunities to deepen and strengthen real friendships are lost. Friendships can be seen as built on shared confidences, and confidences cannot be shared socially. Telling all our friends about the events in our lives using the same words, phrases, and images is like communicating with a bullhorn. And broadcasted information isn't terribly friendly or personal however social it may be. This means that while Facebook or social media in general may have its place, while it may facilitate a certain kind of friendly interaction, it is not personal but social.

21

As such, not only is it not a replacement for personal friendship, it is not much of an enhancement either, providing a merely generic mode of communication while simultaneously taking opportunities away from reaching out personally to friends in more intimate, tailored, and trusting ways.

We often think of friendship as transitive, saying "Any friend of yours is a friend of mine," though we also generally acknowledge the limits of this "transitivity"; it is certainly not logical transitivity. There are friends of friends who we know of and may perhaps have met and even felt friendly toward, yet who are not friends. There are also acquaintances that are not quite friendships, though they may involve friendly feelings of fellowship or solidarity not obtained among strangers. Friendships come in multifarious forms. Aristotle, who wrote at length about friendship and its importance for a well-lived life (books VIII and IX of *Nicomachean Ethics*), noted that some friendships are merely of instrumental value while others are based on something more worthwhile and valuable than that. There are extended debates among contemporary philosophers as to the proper basis for friendship: many think that friends are properly valued for their characterological traits, we value friends who are, for example, wise or courageous; others think that friends are valued for more idiosyncratic reasons, the way friends have quirks or share "inside jokes" or a particular history.[1] The point here need not take sides on such a debate, since all agree that friends are not fungible: we cannot replace one friendship with another or swap friends out for each other keeping the friendship the same. If we lose a friend and gain a new one, the new one may take on some of the roles of the old one, but still it is a new and different friendship. What is important here is the way in which friends interact and the degree to which it is true that since people are unique, their friendships are also unique.

Being friends with someone requires responding to that person in a way that respects their individuality. When we talk about what is going on in our lives with one friend, we tailor what we say to the friend we are talking to. And if we are talking to more than one friend at once, then once again this affects how we communicate, it affects the substance of the communication which affects the uptake of what is said by the listening friend(s). Not only do we tell some of our friends some aspects of our lives which we do not share with others, the words we choose and the manner in which we relate information covaries with the level of intimacy we have with who we are talking to as well with kind of friendship it is. Perhaps we are more apt to talk about family issues with childhood friends who know our families well, perhaps we are more apt to talk about career challenges or successes with those of our friends whose careers are more similar to our own. That isn't to say that we don't talk about our families with our work friends or our careers with our childhood friends, only, rather, that what we say and how we say it will depend on to whom we are talking. These are not meant to be "deep thoughts," just very commonsense thoughts that have consequences for the thesis at hand. Our friendships are not all cut from the same piece of cloth, nor should we want them to be: our lives are richer for the variety of our friendships.

One way to gauge friendships or even "order" them is by how psychologically intimate we are with our friends, how much of our lives we are willing to share. Few, if any, know everything about us. Perhaps our very best friends and/or our spouses know practically everything there is to know about us. Some have even argued (unpersuasively to my mind) that since quality of friendship depends on how much we disclose to them, we can only have one best friend, to whom we maximally disclose, at a time (Thomas 1987). Regardless of whether or not we accept such arguments as sound, it is intuitive that our better friends know more about us, about our inner lives—our joys and fears—than mere acquaintances and that there is something proper and correct about this. We do not share information about ourselves in an egalitarian way, we say more to some and less to others and the situation or the circumstances of who is listening affects what we say and how we say it. Nor do we listen and respond in the same way to our friends when they are sharing information about themselves regardless of who else is around. It may make sense to criticize a friend in private when doing so in public would be quite unfriendly; we may speak, listen, and behave differently at a large party, a small dinner party, or at a tête-à-tête. And responding to these differences of local and company together with our friends can itself deepen a friendship. In all these ways, and for all these reasons, we differentiate between our friends, and our friendships taken on unique characteristics. Our friendships are at least as different as the personalities of our friends.

Now, on Facebook, we can communicate with our friends in a one-on-one way or with some sub-group of friends. This is similar to how we can write emails to as many people at a time as we like. While telephoning is normally a two-person conversation, it need not be. Insofar as we use these "tailored" aspects of Facebook's functionality, so that we are selecting who we communicate with from all our friends, writing our messages to that particular collection of friends, then Facebook is a fine venue to pursue our friendships, similar to other forms of written communication.[2] When we communicate with particular people, choosing our words and our modes of expression to suit those with whom we are communicating, our communication is personal. But this is not characteristic of Facebook. What is striking about it is that all of our friends are grouped together, our best friends with our acquaintances with those who are merely friends of friends whom we hope may one day become actual friends. And what we post, we characteristically post to all. And the numbers of people involved are typically quite large, far larger than the number of friends that people would have considered as their "friends" before social media existed. Despite how many actual friends people have in "real life," they often have hundreds of friends on Facebook and some have thousands. Indeed, half of all adult Facebook users have more than 200 "friends" and 42 percent of men and 50 percent of women cite the ability "share with many people at once" as a "reason for using Facebook" (Smith 2014).

So, let's distinguish communication which is individualized or tailored to the particular people to whom it is directed from communication which is generic, or written in such a way that it is for "mass consumption." Some of the ways in which communication can be tailored have already been discussed. Generic communication is the way we express ourselves when we are speaking to large groups of people whose only link to each other is the fact that we are communicating with them. We communicate in these ways when we make invitations, or when we make toasts or speeches at an event, or when we are generically announcing news, such as a betrothal or a birth or a death. Generic speech is for some portion of the general public, often we do not care all that much who hears it: it is not personal, but is social, in the sense of "social" that is at play in "social media." Rather than a tête-à-tête, Facebook is a form of "mass communication."

The point is not that there is something wrong or bad about Facebook. Facebook is something like being at a party with everyone you know and often with people who only know who you know. And of course, there is nothing wrong with parties, nothing wrong with large groups. Friendships can even be strengthened by the friends going to parties together or by gathering in large groups. The point is rather that if this is the primary sort of situation in which we meet with our friends, then we cease to have much personal contact with any of them. We meet them en masse, not as individuals, but as a social group. And if this is the only way to interact with them, our friendships will indeed suffer.

This is so for the reasons that are characteristic of the sort of generic communication which was just introduced. When we communicate with a large group of people, we present information in a way that is accessible to all of them. There are no "inside jokes," no references to shared experiences, no way to situate the message into a common history or to contextualize it so that it has any special meaning for the person who is reading or hearing the communication. We cannot try to explain what happened to us by way of analogy with something that we know happened to the person to whom we are talking. The communication is not personal, but social; speaking to a group, even a friendly group, is different than speaking to an individual just as speaking to a sibling is different than speaking to the entire family. The communication necessarily becomes, in a sense, flatter in content, less nuanced. Details which are more personal, more confidential, more private are left out. While one may have confidence in a group, it is of a different sort than confidence in an individual; we typically take only individuals "into our confidences" and trusting a group is not like trusting an individual. These "flavors" of confidence and trust are hard to pull apart from a phenomenological point of view, though, with groups, the content of the communication involved will be more "abstract" in the early sense of word, when taken as a verb and meaning "to remove" or "extract," to "withdraw," literally "to move away." While "oversharing" is a new but quickly popular word, and complaining that one is being given "too much information" is so common that it has an acronym, even then, oversharing communication still has less personal content, less tailoring, than how that same information would be conveyed to a single, dear friend. It is almost hard to imagine writing a letter to a special friend, communicating some important life event, and writing a second letter to all one's friends and acquaintances about the same news, and having the letters end up being identical in word or even tone. Similarly, it would be odd indeed if a person spoke about an important matter in the same way to an individual friend as to a group, and, were it to happen, we would think the friendship involved was superficial at best.

TRUST AS A RELATIONSHIP OF THREE TERMS

Trust can be understood as a relationship of three terms: X trusts Y with Z (Baier 1986). And while we can trust different people, as individuals and/or groups, with the same thing, the manner of our trust or the degree to which we trust will vary according to the quality of the relation between the trusting person and the trustee(s). The more valuable Z is the greater the degree of trust X must place in Y. People can overshare, yes, but no one posts their social security number or credit card information online. And personal information, about our deep emotional states, about our fears and our hopes, is of great psychological value to us. This does not mean that we ought to keep private the most important things about us, or keep them as secrets. Nor is there anything wrong with making (even large amounts of) personal information public. But if people may post their most intimate thoughts and feelings, which may only be truly apt for a private diary, there is a sense in which this sort of shamelessness is quite foolish. There is a difference between an honest person's "having nothing to hide" and being willing to share everything with everyone. Trying to be everyone's friend means that one will be no one's friend; indeed, being too trusting of others demonstrates a lack of untrustworthiness, a lack of discretion or care with what is valuable. Even if it is possible to have more than a single best friend, it is certainly impossible to have a hundred of them. If one is not able to discriminate between what may and what should not be shared about oneself, then one doesn't show to others that their confidences will be kept. These are, again, not meant to express deep thoughts, but to show extremes of communicative behavior which are easy to spot as not being conducive to friendship in any meaningful sense.

So, what are the norms? How trustworthy is the information one learns online? What does it say about us that we are so willing to grab the bullhorn? There is some reason to think that truthfulness takes a hit. The data seem to suggest that we are more likely to shade or spin the truth or pad it when we communicate online than when we do face to face. Research by Jeffrey Hancock (2007) indicates that people lie more frequently online than they do face to face, and that lying is most widespread in media that is synchronous, recordless, and distributed. One reason for this is that it is easier to get away with lying online than it is in real life: there is a "motivational impairment effect" suggesting that most of the time, in real life, the more motivated the liar, the higher the likelihood of detection, while Hancock found the opposite to be true with computer mediated communication (CMC); that is, that there is a "motivational enhancement effect" in lying in CMC: the more motivated the online liar is, the harder it is to detect the lie. And even if people are not lying, other research by Joseph Walther indicates that people often "exploit the technological aspects of CMC in order to enhance the messages they construct to manage impressions and facilitate desired relationships" (Walther 2007). How we present ourselves is of great importance to us, and the ability to control exactly how and when information is disseminated in social media allows us to be quite selective in our word choice, editing behavior, sentence complexity, etc., and much of this depends on how "desirable" our intended audience is. In an interview with Susan Dominus of the *New York Times*, Randi Zuckerberg, the sister of the founder of Facebook Mark Zuckerberg, responded to the question "What are you most guilty of on Facebook?" by saying:

> I'm a marketer, and sometimes I almost can't take it out of my personal life. I've had friends call me and say, "Your life looks so amazing." And I tell them: "I'm a marketer; I'm only posting the moments that are amazing." (2013)

Even if, as a marketer, Mr. Zuckerberg takes this practice to an extreme, it seems likely that everyone does this to one degree or other. Even if we are posting bad news, we are presenting it in a particular way, a way in which we are most comfortable with all our "friends" seeing it. We almost invariably "hide the warts," and communicate in a way that paints us in as flattering a light as possible. Such biased self-presentation maybe endemic to humanity, indeed, we may even be self-deceived by our own biased self-presentations in social media.[3] Regardless, in all cases, we are often likely to present ourselves in as positive a light as we can muster, though this "spinning" is far more easily supported by social media than by personal, face-to-face interaction.

When posting on Facebook in the characteristic way, that is by broadcasting news of our personal lives to all our "friends" at once, this says something about the way we are willing to present ourselves to people, to draw the attention of a great many people to ourselves at once. There is something naturally exhibitionist about such large-scale voluntary disclosure; consider the rise of the "selfie." In our normal lives, while there may always be some extroverts or lovers of attention whose behavior says, "Look at ME!" this tone infuses all characteristic Facebook posting. While privacy, introversion, and shyness are all perfectly consistent with genuine friendship, there is far less, if any of this, on Facebook. This has led some to a great deal of speculation and research on the relationship between social media and narcissism. While obviously such theorizing will be contentious, there is a commonsense connection to be seen between repeating actions which scream "Look at ME!" and a rise of narcissism.[4] Research indicates that while use of Twitter supports the superiority aspect of narcissism (a "snarkier than thou" attitude), Facebook supports the exhibitionist aspects of narcissism (Panek, Nardis, and Konrath 2013). This is not to claim that social media actually causes narcissism, but there is some research which does suggest this (Wilcox and Stephen 2013). For example, people who undergo blows to their ego are more likely to use Facebook (Toma and Hancock 2013).

This is not to argue that the billions of people are on Facebook are all nascent narcissists or incipient egocentrics. What these thoughts should do is make us be wary of how social media is affecting our genuine friendships. We do not count on our friends to only see the good or even best aspects of ourselves and our lives. Rather, the better our friends, the more we want them to see us truly, for who we are. This is both because most people prefer to be liked and accepted for who they are and not for merely how they superficially and misleadingly might appear, and also because we count on our friends to help us improve ourselves, to criticize us (gently!) when it is most apt, and to give accurate and helpful feedback on what happens in our lives. Our genuine friendships are damaged to the degree that social media allows or even encourages us to distort the image of ourselves we project to the world, our best friends along with our acquaintances. Even if there is a population of people out there who is not affected in any adverse way by these idiosyncrasies of social media, such that they use Facebook in, shall we way, a perfectly virtuous way, it seems likely this will be a minority, while the rest of us will be negatively affected whether we realize it or not.

CONCLUSION

Consider that the average active Facebook user spends seven hundred minutes a month on the site (Kissmetrics 2014). Now, imagine that same amount of time, or some large percentage of it, spent individually writing or talking to genuine friends in direct one-on-one or very small group situations. Can there be any doubt which will lead to better friendships? The argument here is not the "time displacement argument" about how much time Facebook may take away from friendship.[5] Data seem to indicate that time spent on Facebook is time that would otherwise be spent on watching television or other non-friendly activities. Rather, the way in which Facebook may harm a friendship is by usurping opportunity costs: imagine some good news arrives and can be shared with an individual personally or with that same individual socially through Facebook. If the news is shared personally, this arguably affects the friendship in a more positive way than if it is shared socially; it will mean more to your friend if you make the effort to send a special personal message, than to read the same thing along with everyone else. So, Facebook may not be outright harmful to friendship, though it may get in the way of friendships developing as much as they could. Facebook is certainly not the best way to deepen friendships in a way that is most rewarding and leads to best-lived life. But regardless, however, perhaps all this is only shaking a fist at the wind, since everything discussed here is the "new ordinary" (McKinney, Kelly, and Duran, 2012).[6]

NOTES

1. For a defense of repeatable traits as the basis of friendship, see, for example, Jennifer Whiting, "Impersonal Friends" in *Monist*, 1991, 74: 3–29; for the contrary position, see, for example, Neera Badhwar, "Why It Is Wrong to Be Always Guided by the Best: Consequentialism and Friendship," *Ethics*, 1991, 101: 483–504.

2. One might think that it is the written aspect of Facebook that hampers friendship, especially if the alternative is to meet with someone face to face and to talk verbally. Clearly, it seems that "face-time" is better than Facebook. But people have been maintaining friendships through writing as long as there has been mail, and penpals can be friends even though they have never met. So, while talking is probably easier and preferable to writing, especially since it allows for eye contact and other forms of expressed emotion, perhaps surprisingly, these do not seem to be necessary to friendship. The point here is that while face-time may not be necessary for friendship, individualized communication, as opposed to generic contact, is necessary.

3. See my "Social Media, Self-Deception, and Self-Respect," in *Social Media and the Value of Truth*, M. Haney and B. Beasley (eds.) (Lanham: Lexington Books), 2013.

4. See, for example, papers cited below. For a contrary view, see Keith Hampton, Lauren Sessions Goulet, Cameron Marlow, and Lee Rainie, "Why Most Facebook Users Get More than They give," in *Pew Internet*, February, 3 2012, at www.pewinternet.org/Reports/2012/Facebook-users/Summary.aspx?view=all; see also "Narcissism or Openness?: College Students' Use of Facebook and Twitter" by Bruce McKinney, Lynne Kelly, and Robert L. Duran (2012) in *Communication Research Reports* 29(2): 108–118.

5. See Shannon Vallor, "Flourishing on Facebook: Virtue Friendship and New Social Media," *Ethics and Information Technology*, 2012, 14(3): 185–199.

6. While I know she disagrees with me about the present thesis, I would like to thank Alexis Elder for many instructive conversations about friendship and comments on a draft of this paper.

REFERENCES

Baier, A. (1986). "Trust and Anti-Trust." *Ethics* 96: 231–260.

Dominus, S. (2013, November 1.) "Randi Zuckerberg: 'I really put myself out there.'" Retrieved from www.nytimes.com/2013/11/03/magazine/randi-zuckerberg-i-really-put-myself-out-there.html?partner=rss&_r=0.

Hancock, J. (2007). "Digital Deception: Why, When and How People Lie Online," in *Oxford Handbook of Internet Psychology*, eds. K. McKenna, T. Postmes, U. Reips, and A. N. Joinson. Oxford: Oxford University Press.

Kissmetrics. (2014, February 6). Facebook Statistics. Retrieved from http://blog.kissmetrics.com/facebook-statistics/.

McKinney, B., Kelly, L., and R. L. Duran. (2012). "Narcissism or Openness?: College Students' Use of Facebook and Twitter." *Communication Research Reports* 29, 2: 108–118.

Panek, E., Nardis, Y., and S. Konrath. (2013) "Mirror or Megaphone? How Relationships between Narcissism and Social Networking Site Use Differ on Facebook and Twitter." *Computers in Human Behavior* 29, 2004–2012.

Smith, A. (2014, February 6). "6 New Facts about Facebook." Retrieved from www.pewresearch.org/fact-tank/2014/02/03/6-new-facts-about-facebook/.

Toma, C. L., and J. T. Hancock. (2013). "Self-Affirmation Underlies Facebook Use. *Personality and Social Psychology Bulletin* 39(3): 321–31.

Thomas, L. (1987). "Friendship." *Synthese* 72: 217–36.

Walther, J. B. (2007). "Selective Self-Presentation in Computer-Mediated Communication: Hyperpersonal Dimensions of Technology, Language, and Cognition." *Computers in Human Behavior* 23: 2538–2557.

Wilcox, K., and A. Stephen. (2013). "Are Close Friends the Enemy? Online Social Networks, Self-Esteem, and Self-Control." *Journal of Consumer Research*. DOI: 10.1086/668794.

FOUR

The Duplicity of Online Behavior

Joseph Ulatowski

People commonly believe that any form of deception, no matter how innocuous it is and no matter whether the deceiving person intended it otherwise, is always morally wrong. In this chapter, I argue that deceiving in real time is morally distinguishable from deceiving online because online actions are not as morally innocuous as actions occurring in real time. Our failure to detect the fine-grained characteristics of a virtual avatar, which refers to the personality associated with a screen name, leads us to believe that the person intended to do a moral harm. Openly deceiving someone on Facebook or Twitter is not a way to build wholesome virtual friendships but to destroy them. This chapter addresses how the traditional philosophical understanding of the doing/allowing harm distinction fails to apply in cyberspace.[1]

INNOCUOUS PASSIVE DECEPTION

Some examples of deception we commonly employ in our lives do not yield a moral harm. If the consequences of these forms of deception are not morally wrong, then we have to entertain the possibility that online actions of virtual avatars are not morally harmful. Online deception lacks some of the characteristics of real time deception, and without these characteristics, online deception cannot help but be morally harmful.

Suppose Alma and Bonita are deeply in love and have been together a very long time. They have such a close emotional bond that each knows the other would never do anything to harm their relationship. One morning Alma and Bonita decide they should treat themselves to a night of

31

dinner and dancing. Both agree to meet for dinner at 6:00 p.m. Alma arrives at the restaurant around 5:50 p.m. only to discover that Bonita has not yet arrived. The maître d' seats Alma, after which she sends a text message asking Bonita when she will arrive. Bonita, who is in a business meeting with colleagues that will likely not end for another ten minutes, responds with the following message: "OTW," which is text speak for "on the way." Although, in fact, Bonita is not on the way to meet Alma, her text's content expresses to Alma that she is, implying Bonita has deceived Alma.

We ought not to think Bonita harmed Alma, even though Bonita clearly deceived Alma into believing she was on her way to the restaurant. Conversationally, in text speak, "OTW" means not only that a person is physically moving toward a particular destination but also that one will be on the way shortly, one is on the way but ran into someone on the way of out the door, or—perhaps as is more frequently the case in larger metropolitan areas—one is stuck in pedestrian or vehicle traffic and should arrive shortly.

Despite these alternative meanings to "OTW," what Bonita has texted to Alma is what one might call a bald-face lie. Bonita is in the meeting. She's not walking out the door. She's not stuck in traffic. She's not even intending to leave the meeting early to meet with Alma for the dinner they'd planned earlier in the day. So, the alternative understandings of "OTW" do not apply in this case.

Further evidence seems to rule against a charitable reading of Bonita's text message. There is no doubt Bonita will be on her way as soon as the meeting ends ten minutes hence. The trouble is that the form of the text message suggests she's on her way to meeting Alma right now. Texting Alma that she's "OTW" suggests to Alma that Bonita is "walking" or "driving" toward the restaurant. The use of an acronym in place of the phrase, "On the way," suggests the text was sent in haste with some urgency. Moreover, it triggers in Alma's mind that she should not follow up that message with another because it could distract Bonita, whether she's driving or walking to the restaurant.[2]

Suppose the story were to continue in the following way: Bonita arrives thirty minutes late to the restaurant and pleads with Alma to forgive her for being so tardy. Bonita's telling Alma where she was when she texted does not improve Alma's thinning patience, but, perhaps surprisingly, Alma is not quite angry with Bonita for making her wait. The idea that Bonita could have called Alma before the meeting began warning her of a belated arrival might not have even crossed Alma's mind. Instead, she's happy to see Bonita and looking forward to dinner with her. However, for instance, if Alma discovered that Bonita had been unfaithful or that Bonita had drained her bank accounts and moved to Acapulco, Alma probably would not have been as forgiving as she was this evening. Why is this? In the example, Bonita lied to and deceived Alma.

In some cases we seem to overlook deception, while in others it's difficult to turn a blind eye to it.

The case of Alma and Bonita is just one way in which we deceive our closest friends, spouses, or siblings using social networking platforms, such as texting.[3] The deception did not result in harming either Alma or Bonita, but what Bonita did was morally wrong if we believe that we ought not lie to others, especially if it as self-serving as the lie Bonita told Alma.

Perhaps one would not want to call what Bonita did an act of lying. She might have overlooked the fact that her meeting might continue for thirty minutes. In one commonly held definition, lying is the act of making a false statement with the intention to deceive (Kagan 1998). Since Bonita may not have intended to deceive Alma, she did not lie to her. We might even say that Bonita did not deceive Alma. Regardless, overlooking a particular fact seemingly frees Bonita from any moral wrongdoing because she did not intend to deceive Alma. Given that no moral harm resulted from Bonita's text, we judge her passive act of deception to be harmless and innocuous.

INNOCUOUS ACTIVE DECEPTION

In the previous section, we were introduced to a real time example, that is, one commonly occurring in the actual world amid practical affairs, where a person's deception did not result in any kind of moral harm. So, we concluded that the act involved no moral wrongdoing. We might call such cases "innocuous passive deception." A critic might contend that such innocuous actions that involve no moral wrongdoing are not forms of deception. The critic might also maintain that all forms of deception yield harmful or painful results, so those sorts of actions that fail to fit into such a category must not be a form of deception.

In this section, I will argue there are active forms of deception that fail to be a case of moral wrongdoing. Despite the critic's conception of deception always involving a moral harm and moral wrongdoing, these examples of active deception are just as innocuous and morally inert as the example of Alma and Bonita. Once I have shown that innocuous forms of active deception involve no moral wrongdoing, I will be able to discuss cases of online deception that do not divide easily between innocuous and egregious forms of active and passive deception. If this is true, then the kind of nuance our real time behaviors permit do not translate into permissible online behaviors. We ought to, then, refrain from performing any action online that could be understood as an egregious and morally harmful action.

One might believe, as the critic appears to, that as opposed to the moral inertness of innocuous passive deception, it must be the case that all forms of active deception are morally harmful and, therefore, a good example of moral wrongdoing. There are cases of active deception which do not clearly show the action to be a moral wrongdoing. The singular feature that stands out in these active forms of deception is that the agent acted intentionally. The agent intended to lie or to deceive others. Because of this, we might believe that it is morally wrong.

Some deceptive acts are undertaken (and intentionally so) not to harm others but to protect others (and oneself) from harm. Soldiers, for example, wear camouflage uniforms to hide from and to deceive enemy combatants. Some camouflage is more effective than other forms of camouflage because it enables soldiers to blend in with the elements of the environment. Deceiving enemy soldiers by using camouflage preserves opponent soldiers from harm, and not wearing camouflage, especially in light of strategies adopted in modern warfare (for example, guerrilla tactics), could mean certain death.[4] I believe it goes without saying that wearing camouflage is not morally wrong; in fact, one might go so far as to contend that not wearing camouflage in battle is reckless and, therefore, possibly morally forbidden.

Besides the use of camouflage in war time, there are other forms of innocuous active deception. Think of the boss who lays off an employee because the employee always submits work after institution-wide deadlines. When the boss "fires" the employee (after filing the appropriate paperwork, of course), she might tell the employee that "the company has terminated the position you occupy" or "the company's moving in a different direction." Eliminating a position in the company is not the same as "firing" the employee because the employee might believe the company can no longer afford to pay for the skills he possesses. In a sense, the employee does not feel that the company or administrators have "fired" him but that the company can no longer afford the services the employee provides. Of course, the boss actively deceived the (now ex-) employee because it was the employee's failure to submit material on time that brought about the "separation."

Despite the outright deception perpetrated by the employer in this case, our reaction to it might not be to ascribe some sense of moral wrongdoing to the employer; instead, our intuition tells us that the employer seemingly has preserved and protected the employee's psyche. No moral harm comes to the employee. Thus, there seems little reason to think that what the employer has done is morally wrong.

Perhaps in reading the above examples one might conclude that innocuous active deception is found in circumstances where the agent justifies a certain means to reach a highly beneficial end. If there are other more intimate settings in which active deception arises, then we might be less dismissive of deception.

There are, in fact, intimate settings in which active deception seems to occur. Many of them focus on relationships in families. Suppose a parent takes away a toy from a child because it is too loud, but the parent tells the child that the toy is broken. The toy is not broken, but the parent intentionally deceives the child so that he does not have to listen to the loud toy any longer. No moral harm comes to the child, even if the child really wants to play with the toy that has been taken away. In this example, the parent intends to deceive the child by telling her that the toy is broken and is no longer fit for play, even though the parent knows the toy is in perfect working order.

Similarly, think of the parent who tells a child that "Santa Claus will not be bringing her any toys this Christmas because she's been a naughty little girl." This is doubly deceiving. First, there is no Santa Claus to bring gifts to the little girl. Santa Claus is a fictitious entity. The parent has perpetuated a lie about the existence of a being that does not actually exist. Second, the deceit seems a way for parents to get what they want from the child. In this instance, they are treating the child merely as a means to an end. Acting nice, the child will get what she wants and the parents will get what they want, which is perhaps a better behaved child. The parents telling the child Santa will not be delivering presents to her is doubly deceiving, but it is a common tactic parents use to get what they want from a child.

At this point, I have introduced examples occurring in real time that seem to show there are morally innocuous forms of active and passive deception. The question with which we will be concerned in the next two sections is whether active and passive deception occurring online and in virtual social worlds is equally morally innocuous. It is my contention that the conditions for active and passive deception do not easily translate from the real time world to the virtual world. Netizens ought to exercise greater care in their deceptive behavior than they would in real time affairs because online behaviors have real time consequences, some of which—unfortunately, as we have witnessed—can be catastrophic.

ONLINE DECEPTION: INNOCUOUS OR DANGEROUS?

There is a widespread belief that the real time world and the virtual world are completely distinct. We live life differently in each, and we believe that the things we say and do in the virtual world do not carry over to the real time world. In the previous section, I set out to show that there are innocuous forms of active and passive deception. For this section, I will briefly illustrate why we believe the online virtual world and the real time world are distinguishable. Then, I will show that our belief in this distinction is wrong. An argument for this view will come later in the chapter in a discussion of doing something versus letting something happen. Finally, in the last section, I will show how virtual world deception, whether active or passive, yields seriously harmful consequences. If

my analysis is correct, then we should refrain from deceiving others online.

There is a distance between us and virtual netizens that permit us to
do and to say things that we would not normally do or say to people on
the street. When the internet began to take shape and online interactions
were more common toward the end of the 1990s, I can remember entering a chat room named "Philosophy" or "Nietzsche on Value." I presumed that we would have a discussion about the chatroom's title. Sometimes the discussion was fruitful, but most of the time it was not. Online
chat rooms had the tendency to devolve into school playground arguments. Arguments would amount to "yah-huh" and "nun-uh." What
should have passed for an enlightening chat became nothing interesting
whatsoever.

There is at least one reason why schoolyard arguments take place in
online forums. The discussants use anonymous handles. Anonymity provides them the opportunity to use baseless claims and offer unguarded
opinions. The degeneration of the discussion might have been avoided if
members of the chatroom had not anonymized their own profiles. Profiles, at least in the 1990s, were easy to anonymize. Discussants could
easily cloak their own identity. For example, the only thing known about
the person chatting was their handle, "fideo1991" or "veritasetvirtus."
Handles typically do not provide an adequate amount of information to
identify the handle with any person.

There was no other place people could be as anonymous as they were
when they were online. This is true today, too. Look at any *New York
Times* editorial generating interest and comments among its readers, and
it is easy to find a few anonymous commentators posting ugly opinions
surreptitiously.

Fast forward to the current era of social networking sites like Facebook or LinkedIn. Although it is not recommended, one can create fictitious Facebook or Twitter accounts. A person is capable of manipulating
one's online identity in a way he or she is unable to do in real time. A
person wandering around town in a mask would likely garner some
attention from not only ordinary people but the local authorities as well.
Given that manipulation of one's identity is so easy to do online, this
seems to be one underlying reason why we believe the online world and
the real time world are distinct.

Clandestine interactions online have a far greater possibility of going
undetected than secret meetings in real time. No matter what it is a person does in real time there is a chance the encounter will be filmed by
closed-circuit televisions, that the NSA is watching, or the encounter is
being surveyed by a private investigator. Even if the person wears a
costume, mask, wig, or fake mustache, the existence of facial recognition
software or other means of identifying a person will give away the person's true identity. No such luck online. It seems possible to cruise the

internet undetected without any repercussions for the individual who covertly engages in nefarious and illicit affairs.

For these reasons, I believe culture has disentangled the world wide web from the web of humanity. No longer do we believe that our online behavior has any serious consequences, good or bad, in real time. The trouble is that our online behavior does have consequences.

There have been tragic consequences resulting from the creation and maintenance of fake social networking profiles. Megan Meier, a thirteen-year-old girl suffering from depression and attention deficit disorder, committed suicide after a "fake" person she began corresponding with on MySpace ended their friendship. It was discovered later that the "fake" person's profile had been set up by neighborhood bullies who berated Megan in chats on the once popular social networking site. In another incident, Brandon Wentzell consumed a lethal cocktail of vodka and Dilaudid after his long-distance Facebook girlfriend, Clarissa Chistiakov, canceled an in-person meeting and discontinued the relationship they had fostered. It turns out that Clarissa did not exist.

The consequences of any action can be either good or bad. Whenever we consider deceitful behavior, we think the outcome will be bad for whatever agent is the victim of the deceit. Online behavior seems to make one more prone to being a victim of bad action because of the anonymity involved in online interactions. If it is possible for us to refrain from behaving badly online and to prevent bad things from happening to other members of the social network, then we have a moral obligation to prevent unnecessary suffering of our fellow internet users (Singer 1972). Not doing anything seems tantamount to permitting bad things to happen to innocent cyber-bystanders.

Now that I have argued for the view that the real time world is not easily distinguished from the online world, I can move on and discuss one way in which we might justify to ourselves why we let certain things happen on the internet we would not otherwise allow in real time. We believe there is some spatial distance between us and other cyber-travelers. If no such distance justifies treating others differently online, then we must cautiously approach the distinction between doing and allowing online. Since the doing/allowing relationship resembles the connection between active/passive deception, we also have reason to give up such a distinction online.

DOING VS. ALLOWING HARM

It seems intuitively obvious that doing some harmful act is morally worse than allowing some harmful act to occur. No matter how clear our intuitions may seem to be, controversy over the question, "Is doing harm morally worse than merely permitting harm to occur?" still remains. Suppose a doctor may save six innocent people only if he takes the vital organs, such as the heart, lungs, liver, and kidneys, from a healthy prisoner. To do so the doctor will have to end the prisoner's life. This seems like a morally reprehensible act.

For a second case consider this: Instead of the doctor having to terminate the prisoner's life, suppose that the prisoner is allowed to die. The doctor refrains from putting the prisoner on a life support system. After the prisoner's brain ceases functioning he performs the surgery to save six people's lives. Our intuitions tell us that the second scenario seems to be less morally problematic than the first one.

Permitting a person to die in order to save six people seems less problematic than deliberately ending a person's life in order to save six people. There are numerous ways to account for the distinction between doing and allowing (Bennett 1966, 1993; Dinello 1971; Lichtenberg 1982; Steinbock and Norcross 1994), of which the most sophisticated analysis is Warren Quinn's (1989). Quinn has argued that the distinction between doing and allowing harm depends on whether an agent's most direct contribution is an action or inaction.

> Harmful positive agency is that in which an agent's most direct contribution to the harm is an action, whether his own or that of some object. Harmful negative agency is that in which the most direct contribution is an inaction, a failure to prevent the harm. (Quinn 1989, 301f)

Quinn explains that an agent's most direct contribution to a harmful upshot of his agency is the contribution that most directly explains the harm. And one contribution explains harm more directly than another if the explanatory value of the second is exhausted in the way it explains the first (Quinn 1989, 301).

The primary difference is between cases where an agent produces the harm by an action and cases in which an agent produces the harm by inaction. Ending the prisoner's life is an action, and refraining from putting the prisoner on life support is an inaction. Since ending the prisoner's life is an action and is the contribution that most directly explains the harm, the agent, in Quinn's view, is positively relevant to a harmful upshot. Therefore, ending the prisoner's life is worse than refraining from putting the prisoner on life support.

Quinn offers a range of cases in his Rescue scenarios (1989) to show that the distinction between doing and allowing harm depends on the agent's most direct contribution being an action. In Rescue I, an agent may choose to save five people in danger of drowning or the agent may choose to save one person. The agent cannot save all six. If the agent decides to save the five people at the expense of the one person, the agent's most direct contribution to the one person's death is an inaction. Since the agent has not acted in a way that contributes directly to the one person's death, the agent has not "done" anything to harm the person.

In Rescue II, however, an agent can only save five people by driving over and—presumably—killing one person. The agent's saving five people contributes directly to the death of the one person. So, the agent's most direct contribution is an action, and in this case a "doing."

Quinn contends that there are special cases where an agent may be positively relevant to a harmful upshot, even though the agent's most direct contribution may be characterized as inaction. His example, called Rescue III, is:

> We are off by special train to save five people who are in imminent danger of death. Every second counts. You have just taken over from the driver, who has left the locomotive to attend to something. Since the train is on automatic control you need do nothing to keep it going. But you can stop it by putting on the brakes. You suddenly see someone trapped ahead on the track. Unless you act he will be killed. But if you do stop, and then free the man, the rescue mission will be aborted. So you let the train continue. (Quinn 1989, 298)

The person has not done anything to "let the train continue." Because on Quinn's account the train may act as the person's agent, the person killed the man on the tracks.

Despite that the agent of Rescue III has done nothing, it is the agent's failure to act that makes us believe the person is morally culpable. Quinn argues:

> In this case it seems to me that you make the wrong choice. You must stop the train. It might seem at first that this is because you occupy, if only temporarily, the role of the driver and have therefore assumed a driver's special responsibility to drive the train safely. But, upon reflection, it would not make much moral difference whether you were actually driving the train or merely had access to its brake. Nor would it much matter whether you were in the train or had happened upon a trackside braking device. The important thing from the stand-point of your agency is that you can stop the train and thereby prevent it from killing the one. (Quinn 1989, 299)

Because the agent of Rescue III failed to stop the train, though the agent clearly could have done so, Quinn believes that the person has acted wrongly. Not acting, at least in this instance, yields harm to an innocent bystander and therefore ought to be seen as moral wrongdoing.

To get as clear as possible about the role inaction and action play in the distinction between doing and allowing, Quinn presents one final version of the Rescue scenario, Rescue IV. He writes:

> Suppose . . . you are on a train on which there has just been an explosion. You can stop the train, but that is a complicated business that would take time. So you set it on automatic forward and rush back to the five badly wounded passengers. While attending to them, you learn that a man is trapped far ahead on the track. You must decide

whether to return to the cabin to save him or stay with the passengers and save them. (Quinn 1989, 299)

In Rescue IV, as in Rescue III, your inaction will result in the death of the person trapped on the track. The difference between Rescue III and Rescue IV, however, is that in Rescue III the agent intends an action of the train which brings about the trapped person's death. In Rescue IV, no such intention is present. The agent intends no action of the train that ultimately leads to the trapped person's untimely demise.[5] Ultimately:

> In Rescue III, but not in Rescue IV, the train kills the man because of your intention that it continue forward. This implicates you, I believe, in the fatal action of the train itself. If you had no control, but merely wished that the rescue would continue—or if, as in Rescue IV, you had control but no such wish—you would not be party to the action of the train. But the combination of control and intention in Rescue III makes for a certain kind of complicity. Your choice to let the train continue forward is strategic and deliberate. Since you clearly would have it continue for the sake of the five, there is a sense in which, by deliberately not stopping it, you do have it continue. For these reasons your agency counts as positive. (Quinn 1989, 300)

According to Quinn, the moral implication of distinguishing doing and allowing in this way depends on the distinction between negative and positive rights, a view he inherits from Philippa Foot (1967). When an agent's action or inaction is positively relevant to some harmful upshot, the agent has violated someone's negative rights. Positive rights have been violated when an agent's action or inaction is negatively relevant to some harmful consequence. Quinn holds that negative rights must be more strictly enforced than positive rights. So, a violation of an agent's negative rights is worse than a violation of an agent's positive rights. A critical aspect of Quinn's view is that the man on the railroad track has a say about what harm may befall him. If he does not have a say, then an agent's negative rights, something we must uphold more stringently, has been abandoned.

Quinn's primary objective is "to find the formulation of the [doing/ allowing] distinction that best fits our moral intuitions" (Quinn 1989, 288). He believed the distinction is of the greatest general importance because "it enters as a strand into many real moral issues and because it stands in apparent opposition to the most general of all moral theories, consequentialism" (Quinn 1989, 288).

Quinn's four "Rescue" cases seem to speak directly to the concerns raised against forms of online deception. Because netizens are unable to discern whether a person is real or fake and because we do take what others say to us and about us very seriously, we ought to err on the side of caution and believe that the harmful upshot of online actions or inactions is morally wrong. Not alerting other users of a fake social networking profile is undertaken intentionally. The likelihood of harm befalling a fake member's "friends" is increased because the anonymity provided by the profile allows the user to say potentially very harmful comments to unsuspecting members.

When netizens deceive other netizens, tragic results could follow. Even if the netizen "did not mean" for the comments to hasten the death of another person, the harm was allowed to be brought about by the netizen's actions. Just in virtue of that fact, we have to judge the netizen's actions harshly. Clearly, the person bringing about the harmful upshot has done something morally wrong.

This section has outlined a distinction between doing and allowing, according to one of the debate's main contributors, Warren Quinn. Then, I argued that if netizens allow harmful acts to be brought about by their inaction, that is, not alerting others to the deception, we have to say they have done something morally wrong.

ONLINE DECEPTION IS HARMFUL

There are some forms of deception, at least in real time, we cannot do without. The soldier's camouflage is one example. Deception often encountered in the virtual space of social networking fails to protect others in any way. In fact, it seems that online deception is prone to harm others, regardless of whether the deceiving agent meant or intended to do so. In this closing section, I will argue against some potential counterarguments one might provide in response to my argument.

First, a critic might contend that creating fake social networking profiles is morally permissible because it allows the author of the fake profile to express herself openly. This kind of argument presumes that free speech is protected, and, if the person feels that her rights might be violated or she could lose her job by openly criticizing her employer online, she should have the ability to do it pseudonymously. Free speech is protected, but free speech that harms others certainly is not. Just as we would not protect harmful speech acts like yelling "Fire!" in a crowded theater, we should not think harmful conversations bringing about a person's death is something that ought to be protected either.

Second, one might believe that since we can think of the virtual world differently than we think of the real time world, any event resulting from online discussions or comments is coincidental. This is a common excuse bullies use if one of their victims harms his or herself. According to this interpretation, the words did not hurt or bring about the harm to the victim. After all, correlation is not causation. This argument has no merit. To believe that Megan Meier's suicide was not caused by her neighbors creating a false identity and berating her online is to overlook the fact that Megan and "Josh," her supposed online friend, had sown a friendship.

"Josh's" terrible comments led Megan to commit suicide. Her death was no coincidence.

Finally, one could defend the use of online deception to protect oneself from real time harm. If a person creates a fake Facebook profile and befriends his spouse to uncover the spouse's infidelity, then we might think that knowing the truth about the spouse outweighs the deception involved to discover it. Although this seems like a strong argument for the moral permissibility of online deception, the likelihood that it will lead to morally harmful actions is greater than the good that might be produced in learning the truth about one's spouse.

CONCLUSION

There are a variety of examples of real time and online deception. No matter how innocuous online deception might seem and that the deceiving person intended it otherwise or did not mean for some consequence to follow, it is always morally wrong to deceive someone online. In this paper, I have argued that deceiving in real time is morally distinguishable from deceiving online because online actions are not as morally innocuous as actions occurring in real time. Our failure to detect the fine-grained characteristics of another virtual netizen leads us to believe that the person intended to do a moral harm. Openly deceiving someone on Facebook or Twitter is not a way to build virtual friendships but to destroy them and, at least sometimes, to end the life of innocent virtual bystanders.

NOTES

1. I am grateful to Dr. Jane Kaworski and Jim Nico for inviting me on their internet radio show, *The Social Network Show*, where we discussed issues that led me to thinking about the problems associated with online deception and drafting this paper.

2. One might argue that since Bonita is in a business meeting her use of "OTW" is justifiably urgent because she does not want to be disturbed by Alma again. Even if one were to argue that her being in a business meeting justifies Bonita's use of acronyms, it hardly saves her from the charge that she's lied to her close friend, Alma.

3. For purposes of this chapter, I consider all forms of technology that provide us with a greater reach to others a "social network." Not only will the usual suspects be discussed, like Facebook, Twitter, SnapChat, Pinterest, LinkedIn, and so on, but also the less obvious examples of social networking: smartphones, the internet, chatrooms, discussion boards, blogs, and so on. I realize that this is fairly wide definition of social networking with which some might take issue.

4. Conventional war-time strategy where soldiers meet on the battlefield in regular and patterned formation had to be abandoned shortly following the invention of high-velocity automatic weaponry, for example, the machine gun. Too many casualties were suffered because regular formation made the soldier vulnerable to any unskilled marksman. According to legend, for instance, at the Battle of the Somme (1916), an estimated 20,000 British soldiers were killed in the first twenty minutes of the battle by Axis machine gunners who took advantage of the soldiers "going over the top" and

running across the desolate no man's land. With nowhere to run or to hide, German gunners very easily cut down, quite literally, the advancing British.

5. In an interesting variant of Rescue IV relegated to a footnote, Quinn admits that if the agent is "the driver or his designated replacement" who has a special responsibility to see to it that the train not run over and kill people trapped on the tracks, then the agent intends for the action of the train to run over the trapped person on the tracks. Interestingly, Quinn rules out this option because "[i]t does not seem to derive from any supposition that, if you stay with the passengers, you will really be taking the train forward or will somehow be party to the fatal action of the train itself" (Quinn 1989, 299).

REFERENCES

Bennett, J. (1966). "Whatever the Consequences." *Analysis* 26(23).

Bennett, J. (1993). "Negation and Abstention: Two Theories of Allowing." *Ethics* 104: 75–96.

Dinello, D. (1971). "On Killing and Letting Die." *Analysis* 31: 84–86.

Foot, P. (1967). "The Problem of Abortion and the Doctrine of Double Effect." *Oxford Review* 5: 5–15.

Kagan, S. (1998). *Normative Ethics*. Boulder, CO: Westview Press.

Lichtenberg, J. (1982). "The Moral Equivalence of Action and Omission." *Canadian Journal of Philosophy* 8: 19–36.

Quinn, W. (1989). "Actions, Intentions, and Consequences: The Doctrine of Doing and Allowing." *Philosophical Review* 98: 287–312.

Singer, P. (1972). "Famine, Affluence, and Morality." *Philosophy and Public Affairs*. Spring: 229–243.

Steinbock, B. and Norcross, A., eds. (1994). *Killing and Letting Die*. New York: Fordham University Press. Second edition.

FIVE

For Better or For Worse

The Influence of Social Media on Individual Well-Being

Pamela A. Zeiser and Berrin A. Beasley

The old adage states that everything changes and that's especially true for mediated communication. Rapid advances in information and communication technology have brought about the creation of digital social media, which offer anyone with access to the internet the ability to produce and share online information, ideas, opinions, documents, pictures, and videos. Kaplan and Haenlein (2010) define social media as, "a group of internet-based applications that build on the ideological and technological foundations of Web 2.0, and that allow the creation and exchange of User Generated Content." Examples include Facebook, YouTube, Google+, Instagram, LinkedIn, Pinterest, Kickstarter, Reddit, Twitter, Kiva, and Vine. Roughly twenty years ago digital social media didn't exist; today, more than 1.73 billion people worldwide have used social media and 2.55 billion are expected to be using it by 2017 (Bennett 2013). Facebook reported 1.2 billion monthly active users in early 2014 (Kurtzlben 2014). Also in 2014, Twitter reported having 255 million monthly active users who tweeted more than 500 million tweets per day worldwide (Twitter Usage 2014). Those statistics represent an unparalleled change in how people communicate with one another, near and far.

Change is fundamentally the recognition of difference, usually by comparison across time or across subjects or objects, and today's communication technologies are vastly different from those of twenty or more years ago. As Larry Diamond (2012b) points out in *Liberation Technology:*

Social Media and the Struggle for Democracy, we need to remember that major changes in communication have occurred before:

> In the fifteenth century, the printing press revolutionized the accumu-
> lation and dissemination of information, enabling the Renaissance, the
> Protestant Reformation, and the scientific revolution. . . . A century and
> a half ago, the telegraph was (invented). . . . Suddenly the world
> shrank; news that once took weeks to travel across the world could be
> conveyed instantly. (5)

Earlier revolutions in communication provide perspective but do not diminish the fact that we are currently experiencing major shifts in how
individuals communicate. For example, Nielsen's *Social Media Report 2012*
found that "total time spent on social media in the United States across
PCs and mobile devices increased 37 percent to 121 billion minutes in
July 2012, compared to 88 billion in July 2011" (*State of the Media*).

Even if not unprecedented, social media still represent a revolutionary
change in communication between ordinary individuals and are new
tools that may help us live well, or at least better than before its advent.
The first social media platform was TheGlobe.com, which in 1994 allowed users to generate content through sharing information and photographs as well as communicating online. It lasted until 2008, when com-
petition from Facebook and Myspace overwhelmed it (Beasley 2013). Today, online social interactions occur through so many platforms and are
so varied it's difficult to pinpoint exactly when, where, why, and how
social media may impact users. Nonetheless, a wide range of studies
conducted during the past fifteen years indicate that the use of social
media can have both positive and negative effects. Maria Konnikova
(2013) writes that "social networks are a way to share, and the experience
of successful sharing comes with a psychological and physiological rush
that is often self-reinforcing." To that end, the act of actively engaging
with others via social networks by posting on walls and messaging can
increase feelings of belonging and decrease feelings of loneliness; however, the inverse is true when users spend time passively consuming the
content of others. Those users are more likely to have an increased sense
of loneliness and a decreased sense of connection.

A massive psychological experiment by Facebook to explore the concept of emotional contagion further reinforces the impact social media
can have. For one week in 2012, Facebook altered the algorithm used to
determine what information appeared in the newsfeeds of 689,003 users,
restricting the number of posts containing words thought to elicit positive emotions, such as "love" and "nice," for one group and posts containing words thought to evoke negative emotions, such as "hurt" and
"ugly," for another. The results: people shown fewer negative words
tended to write posts with fewer negative words and more positive ones
and people shown fewer positive words tended to write posts with fewer

positive words and more negative ones (Grandoni 2014). While the ethical aspects of this experiment came under hot debate, the findings confirmed that social media use can affect one's well-being.

It's simple to say that social media represent a revolutionary change in communications that improve our well-being, but the reality of the impact is far more complex. This was also the case with previous communication revolutions: when Diamond (2012b) explores the dramatic difference the invention of the telegraph made in communication, he also ties its invention to political change: it was "hailed as a tool to promote peace and understanding," but "what followed was not peace and freedom but the bloodiest century in human history" (5). The existence and popularity of still-evolving social media represent major changes in communication technology and use, but whether that change is for the better or the worse will depend upon how social media is utilized by ordinary users. In this chapter, we explore how social media use improves and detracts from one's physical, emotional, social, economic, and political well-being.

WELL-BEING

One way to assess the impact of social media on our lives, societies, and world is to consider its effect on well-being. Dictionary definitions of well-being remain somewhat vague: "the state of being well, happy, or prosperous; welfare" (Neufeldt and Guralnik 1991, 1516). Philosophically, well-being describes what is good *for* someone or what benefits someone.

Aristotle's concept of flourishing, or happiness, results from practiced, reasoned behavior that allows one to achieve the golden mean or the balance "between two extremes of excess and deficiency" (Patterson and Wilkins 2008, 7). Aristotle's basic idea of flourishing serves as the foundation for more modern philosophical theories of well-being, which include Hedonism, Desire Theories, Objective List Theories, and the Capability Approach. Hedonism emphasizes "the greatest balance of pleasure over pain" while Desire Theories, tied to welfare economics, "see people's well-being as consisting of the satisfaction of preferences or desires, the context of which could be revealed by their possessions." Objective List Theories are those "which list items constituting well-being" (Crisp 2013). The Capability Approach, also the Capabilities Approach, goes beyond the existence of well-being, or welfare, to also consider "the freedom to live a life we value and have reason to value" and that through our capabilities we have "the opportunity . . . to lead a valuable or good life" (Qizilbash 2013, 35). The Capability Approach has earned considerable attention in the social sciences as well as philosophy, resulting in the "human development approach" utilized by United Nations agencies and other international actors, though Robeyns (2011) cautions against viewing the approach as solely for development. Instead, she argues, the approach applies to all types of well-being and "there is conceptually or normatively no reason to restrict its scope" to development.

Disagreements over the categorizations of these theories exist, with all but Desires Theories arguably falling into the category of enumerative theories, which "specify an informative list of contributors to well-being" (Fletcher 2013, 206). Disagreements also exist as to whether enumerative lists should be objective, subjective, or can be mixed. Objective List Theory, for example, is criticized because lists include items regardless of people's feelings toward those items, although Fletcher (2013) and others refute these criticisms. Fletcher's Objective List Theory list of well-being consists of "Achievement, Friendship, Happiness, Pleasure, Self-Respect, and Virtue" (214). Nussbaum's Capabilities Approach list includes "life; bodily health; bodily integrity; sense, imagination, and thought; emotions; practical reason; affiliation; other species; play; and control over one's environment" (Nussbaum 2006, 76–78).

While such lists remain controversial and can contain different (if usually similar) items, the philosophy literature on well-being sets a precedent for the use of enumerative lists—as do literatures, scholars, and practitioners in the social sciences. We, therefore, utilize a list to define well-being for individuals. Just as there is no specific definition of well-being, there is no agreed-upon list of items for assessing or measuring it. We compiled our list (see table 5.1) after reviewing lists available from the philosophy literature, social sciences literature, economics literature, governments and government agencies, and international organizations. All of the aspects on this list interrelate, but can also be explored separately.

While we focus on individual well-being, we recognize there are numerous literatures (and lists) on societal well-being. We also understand that individual and societal well-being interact; the well-being of individuals contributes to societal well-being and vice versa. For example, the ways in which a society is governed determines an individual's access to

Table 5.1. Individual Well-Being

- Physical (basic human needs, health, personal security, etc.)
- Cultural (ethnic and national traditions and values, etc.)
- Economic (employment, job opportunities, etc.)
- Educational (access to education, knowledge, information communication, etc.)
- Emotional (mental health)
- Political (individual rights and freedoms, access to political participation, etc.)
- Satisfaction (self-perceived level of well-being)
- Social (personal relationships, leisure time and activities, etc.)

individual rights and freedoms just as individuals' demands for such rights and freedoms can affect the ways in which a society is governed. Social media can therefore impact the well-being of both individuals and societies, but in this chapter we examine only social media's influence on individual well-being, balancing the breadth and depth of our exploration by focusing on only five of the eight aspects of well-being listed in table 5.1: physical, emotional, social, economic, and political.

SOCIAL MEDIA AND WELL-BEING

Physical Well-Being

Nothing is more fundamental to an individual's physical well-being than life and having one's basic needs met. Some enumerative lists of well-being, such as Fletcher's (2013), assume physical well-being and begin beyond it with aspects such as happiness and pleasure. Those utilized by economists and governments for measuring socio-economic development, however, list physical well-being or more specific aspects of it, including basic human needs. In developed countries, social media is rarely relied upon for basic human needs. In developing countries, however, the explosion of cellphone availability and use—roughly 96 percent of the world's population uses cellphones (Chhabra 2013)—has prompted social media and related-technology applications (apps) that can positively impact physical well-being.

The term ICT4D, or "information and communication technology for development," has come to encompass the many innovations supporting international development, primarily socioeconomic but also human and civil rights. These innovations include "mHealth" technologies, which provide health information via mobile phones. One example is a maternal health program in India offered jointly by Dimagi, CARE, and the Grameen Foundation. Through this program, cellphones and open-source software become available to women and health workers. The software provides "a series of avatars resembling female health workers ask(ing) users questions in Hindi about prenatal care. The avatars can also speak regional languages and dialects." With these ICT4D resources, women and health care workers can better learn about and protect maternal and infant health, enabling a mother to better care for her health and that of her baby's (Chhabra 2013).

Access to safe water is certainly a basic human need—and a challenge for more than 700 million people worldwide. This figure includes those living in urban slums such as Kibera, Kenya. M-Maji is a cellphone app that connects sellers and buyers of water in this Nairobi slum. M-Maji, which means "mobile-water" in Swahili, allows water vendors to create daily advertisements noting their "location, price, and purification method, if any" and incorporates a vendor rating system. Residents of Kibera—an informal settlement that has no water infrastructure—can spend anywhere from one hour to a full day locating and purchasing water, sometimes at prices up to eight times those paid by wealthier Kenyans. The M-Maji app, however, allows them free access to the database of advertisements and ratings as well as the ability to file complaints against vendors via text messages. Complaints about water quality and misleading advertised prices as well as on-the-ground water quality tests are used to adjust vendor ratings; daily expiration and resubmission of vendor ads ensures buyers have updated information about ratings, water safety, and price (Chhabra 2013; M-Maji).

According to the M-Maji website, this effort was an intentional shift from the usual humanitarian efforts regarding water, which generally focus directly on providing water and/or improving water quality. The Stanford University professors and graduate students from the disciplines of political science, medicine, and computer science who together created M-Maji instead chose to address "the information side of the problem." In utilizing information and communication technology to address the problem of water in urban slums and shantytowns, M-Maji started with the premise that:

> communities struggle to locate and evaluate the quality of their water on a daily basis, and the possibility that this lack of information pushes the price of water to be higher than it should be based on supply and demand. Thus, by providing better water information to consumers, we might not only reduce the individual burden of finding clean water, but also put downward pressure on water prices, making clean water affordable and accessible to larger segments of Kibera's population. (M-Maji)

This app thus allows multi-way social communication and becomes a tool allowing people in Kibera to better access water as a basic human need. And, logically, parents who can more quickly and cheaply meet their family's water needs have more time and resources to address nutrition or other aspects of their physical well-being.

While ICT4D resources like M-Maji are examples of ways in which social media can improve physical well-being, we must bear in mind that social media use can also be detrimental to physical well-being as illustrated by the numerous crime stories associated with classified ads listed on Craigslist.com. Search for the words "Craigslist killer" on Google and you may be surprised at the number of people who appear. Philip Markoff is perhaps the most well known. He was arrested in June 2009 on charges of robbing and killing Julissa Brisman, a woman who offered massage services on Craigslist. He was also charged with robbing two other women who offered similar services on Craigslist (McPhee 2010). Also dubbed the Craigslist killer is Miranda Barbour, a nineteen-year-old who confessed to the 2013 stabbing death of a forty-two-year-old man who answered her ad on Craigslist for "companionship" in exchange for $100. They met in her car in a mall parking lot where she told him she was sixteen, giving him the opportunity to change his mind about having sex with her. "Instead, he told me it was OK" (Lysiak 2014). That was when she decided to stab him to death, she told a *Newsweek* reporter, explaining his murder and supposedly others by her as an act of protecting girls from molestation. Yet another example of a person labeled the Craigslist killer is Rashad Moon, who is currently awaiting trial for killing Felix DeJesus III for a Samsung tablet DeJesus offered for sale on Craigslist (Walker 2014).

A compilation of Craigslist-related crimes occurring in April 2014 illustrates a number of ways in which using social media networks like Craigslist can be detrimental to one's physical well-being. *The Daily Dot*, an internet newspaper, collected news reports of "74 different incidents occurring in 27 states and the District of Columbia" in which a Craigslist-related crime was reported or arrest was made. Of the seventy-four incidents, eleven resulted in violence, three of which were death. The most common crimes were assault, robbery, or attempted robbery (Sankin 2014). The seriousness of crimes related to Craigslist and other classified ad websites like Backpage.com and Recycler.com led the East Chicago Police Department to make available its parking lot and lobby for Craigslist transactions (Perez 2014).

Examples of murder or assault represent extreme cases, of course, but nonetheless demonstrate that individuals utilize social media for abuse as well as altruism when it comes to this most fundamental aspect of well-being. ICT4D applications, including mhealth and M-Maji, are thankfully more common uses of social media for physical well-being.

Emotional Well-Being

While physical well-being—life itself—is fundamental, human emotions and qualities such as happiness, reason, and virtue were the starting point for Aristotle's flourishing and many other philosophical inquiries into well-being. Such philosophical inquiries are today joined by psychological, medical, social, commercial, and even governmental attention to the mind-body link and the importance of mental health to individual and societal well-being. In the United States at least, mental health topics are far less taboo than in previous generations and increased communication about mental health happens across a variety of media—including social media.

There are, unfortunately, many tragic examples of ways in which communication via social media has adversely affected individual emotional well-being. One such example is cyberbullying. Both face-to-face bullying and cyberbullying are harmful, but cyberbullying is harder to manage or solve. A child being bullied face to face could, for example, change schools. A child being cyberbullied can never escape the reach of his or her bullies. Cyberbullying can lead to low self-esteem, poor grades, skipping school, and drug or alcohol use (stopbullying.gov).

Megan Meier's suicide in 2006 was one of the earliest cases of it. Considerable attention was given to the subject of cyberbullying after the thirteen-year-old killed herself when a boy she had been corresponding with on Myspace began sending her cruel messages like "Megan Meier is a slut." Six weeks after Megan's death, her parents learned the boy, Josh Evans, had never existed and was instead the creation of a neighborhood mother known to Megan's family ("Parents" 2007). In another extreme case, a twelve-year-old girl committed suicide after as many as fifteen girls bullied her for months through online message boards and texts. Approximately one-fifth of all U.S. teens experience some form of cyberbullying (Stanglin and Welch 2013).

Generally, when thinking of the term cyberbullying, it's in regard to what one person does to another, but perhaps an even more disturbing way in which social media may negatively affect one's well-being is its use by individuals to act out psychological issues such as self-harm and self-trolling. Self-harm refers to any way in which a person physically harms him or herself, such as by cutting or burning. A 2011 study published by *The Lancet* revealed that one in twelve teenagers self-harm (Bell 2014). Social media sites offer places for people to anonymously share their self-harming, commonly on photosharing sites like Tumblr, Instagram, and Imgur. While self-harm is a psychological condition that existed before the internet, social media sharing of it allows those who self-harm to feel as though they're connecting with others who may understand their situation and because it offers a certain amount of privacy, something those who self-harm seek because of the shame of doing so (Bell 2014).

Another psychological condition enabled by social media is self-trolling. In internet slang, a troll is someone who deliberately and anonymously posts inflammatory messages, such as in chat rooms or on blogs, intended to generate emotional responses or disrupt conversation. Self-trolling refers to posting hurtful or critical comments about oneself, either anonymously or through counterfeit accounts. According to a 2012 study by The Massachusetts Aggression Reductions Center, 10 percent of the 617 students interviewed said they had anonymously cyberbullied themselves (Englander 2012). Self-trolling results from and further reinforces low self-esteem and a "damaged sense of self"; children and teenagers more firmly believe negative comments about themselves when seen "in black and white," even if they posted the comments themselves. Their shame is reinforced not only by the self-abusive comments, but the fear of humiliation if their self-trolling is exposed (Winterman 2013).

However, just as social media have been used to bully, the technology is also utilized in anti-bullying efforts and to support emotional well-being. In 2012, Osseo, Minnesota high-school student Kevin Curwick received international attention for his initially anonymous Twitter account @OsseoNiceThings. Curwick created it specifically to counter bullying tweets being sent about his fellow students on another Twitter account and then tweeted anonymous compliments such as "great artist but even better friend" and "puts others before herself." Curwick unknowingly started a movement as students in the United States and other countries followed his example by creating similar positive, anti-bullying Twitter accounts (Seavert 2012).

The Love is Louder movement (@LoveisLouder) is sponsored by actress Brittany Snow, MTV, and The Jed Foundation, which was founded by Phil and Donna Satow after their college-age son Jed committed suicide. Love is Louder has accounts on Twitter, Facebook, and Tumblr. The movements aims to counter bullying and negative self-image as well as other mental health issues and "support(s) anyone feeling mistreated, misunderstood, and alone" on Twitter by tweeting encouraging quotes and statements as well as empowering pictures of individuals who write "Love is louder than" statements on their hands—such as Love is Louder than discrimination, bullying, rejection, fear of diversity, being alone, and so forth (The Jed Foundation: History, Love is Louder: The Movement).

There exist Twitter accounts specifically designed to offer mental health information or indirect support—tweets by individuals, mental health professionals, and government agencies or international organizations. The United States National Institutes of Mental Health (@NIMHgov) tweets daily about research, policy, treatment options, and awareness for mental health issues such as addiction, ADHD, and depression. Others accounts are simply intended to be "feel good." Emergency Cute Stuff (@EmergencyPuppy) sends out daily photos of cute animals, with the sole intent of making followers smile. The owner of the account acknowledges in the account profile that many of the photos come from Reddit, another social media platform. And there also exist Twitter chats on mental health topics, located through the use of hashtags such as #mhsm (mental health and social media).

For all aspects of well-being, but especially for emotional well-being, we should remember the difference between technology and its use—and the importance of understanding what use tells us about ourselves and our children. Winterman (2013) quotes New York University's Dr. Danah Boyd's conclusions from research into cyber self-harm by adolescents:

> I find that most adults want to blame the problems that they see on technology rather than recognize that youth are simply using technology to enact a whole host of social and emotional issues they're facing. . . . Technology mirrors and magnifies the good, bad, and ugly

about everyday life but it's much easier to blame the technology than to look deeper.

Social Well-Being

Social media is, by definition, a mediated representation of social aspects of our lives, and can either enhance our well-being or diminish it depending on how social media is used to express or facilitate social interactions. Paul Bloomfield does an excellent job of exploring the different kinds of friendship experienced through Facebook in another chapter in this book, so we'll limit the scope of this discussion to ways in which social media can influence our romantic and familial relationships, our sense of belonging, and our leisure activities. Just as one's "social life" is related to but different from one's mental health, so is one's social well-being related to but different from one's emotional well-being.

One aspect of social media that generates debate about the ways in which its use affects one's well-being is romantic relationships. Reconnecting with old flames online is a common activity these days, and the ability to share detailed information about one's life and feelings in a seemingly private manner, such as a Facebook chat, is appealing. But it's all too easy to get carried away. Reconnection can lead to harmless flirtation, which can develop into an emotional affair and perhaps even a physical one. Marriage therapist Karen Ruskin defines infidelity as more than a physical relationship, which makes social media perfect for having one. "From a marriage therapist's perspective, it's the secrecy and the intimate connection with another human. A betrayal can be as simple as a sext" (Schorr 2013). There are even social media platforms for married individuals seeking affairs. One such is AshleyMadison.com, a married dating service that uses the slogan, "Life is short. Have an Affair" (AshleyMadison.com 2014).

Whether the person engaging in infidelity via Facebook or any other social media network is enhancing his or her well-being is worthy of exploration all on its own, but it seems safe to say that those being cheated on through social media networks are finding their well-being changed, and not in a positive way. They've expressed feelings of hurt, anger, insecurity, devastation, and shame (Schorr 2013). "Technology gives us more access to private information than we ever had before. As a result, we now see more affairs that are emotional in nature because social media provide platforms for sneaky, attention-getting behavior where a person can escape accountability" (Gummow 2014).

Not all social media reconnections are harbingers of infidelity. Mobile platform dating apps foster romantic relationships of all types and their contribution or damage to well-being is debatable and dependent upon a variety of factors separate from the apps themselves. The Tinder app matches people using their Facebook account information. Swipe right on your phone for yes and left for no when pictures and profile bits are presented as possible matches. The company reported in 2014 that 850 million swipes and 10,000 matches were made every day (Tinder.com). Grindr is a similar app, but designed solely for men. The company describes it as an all-male location-based social network that has 5 million users in 192 countries with 10,000 new users downloading the app daily. Using a phone's geodevice the app locates other male users in close proximity to the user's geographic location and displays pictures of them from nearest to farthest away. Tap on a picture and profile information about that person becomes available as do the options to send pictures, chat, and share locations (Grindr.com).

Major global sporting events show us that dating apps are popular worldwide. During the 2014 World Cup, which began June 12, both Tinder and Grindr were opened and downloaded at higher rates. Brazil was already Tinder's third-largest user base and by June 25 "Tinder ha[d] experienced a 50 percent increase in downloads and use in Brazil fueled by amorous tourists." The number of users opening Grindr in Brazil increased 31 percent from early to late June 2014 (Williams 2014).

In addition to locating dating partners, social media can also be used to connect family members in life-changing ways, as in the case of Amira Ali, a Sudanese refugee living in America who reunited with her daughter after twenty-four years thanks to Facebook. Ali became separated from her six-year-old daughter, mother, and sister after local rebels raided her village in Sudan. After walking in the desert for four days, Ali and her other children reached a refugee camp. Eventually they were granted asylum in the United States and moved to Colorado. In 2013 she was persuaded by a friend to create a Facebook account in hopes of finding lost family members. Her sister, the one Ali thought had died in the war, saw it and contacted her, telling Ali that her lost daughter was alive. In March 2014, Ali reunited with the daughter she thought had died twenty-four years earlier (Rodriguez 2014).

Beyond one-on-one connections, social media is also a tool to access information about a huge variety of community festivals, leisure activities, and special events that meet our individual needs for connection on the group level. In Reno, Nevada, primarily Facebook and blogs are used to promote "Food Truck Fridays" and similar events which gather gourmet food trucks in downtown venues or local parks, along with music and entertainment. Nearby Sparks, Nevada, joined in by offering the "Food Truck Drive-In," which combines a gathering of food trucks with a movie shown in the city's downtown Victorian Square amphitheater—also advertised mainly via Facebook (Reno Street Food 2014; Sparks Food Truck Drive-In 2014).

Food truck owners' use of social media has been credited with increasing social interaction and, thus, well-being. In writing about the Kogi food truck, NPR's Ben Bergman (2009) noted that customers can wait over an hour for service and commented on the resulting "sidewalk interaction": "There's a sight here you don't always see in car-centric L.A.: People hanging out on the sidewalk while eating, socializing and listening to music. It took the virtual world of Twitter to bring about all this face-to-face interaction." "Social media has played a large role in not only making the trucks more accessible, but allowing them to cultivate the crucial element of community" (Sniderman 2011).

Economic Well-Being

Aspects on the list of well-being (table 5.1) interrelate; as noted above, emotional and social well-being interact. So, too, physical well-being depends upon employment and other features of economic well-being, just as economic well-being depends upon being healthy enough to be economically productive. Economic survival and stability are less likely to appear in philosophical lists of well-being, and much more likely to appear in lists utilized by social scientists and practitioners such as government and international organization officials. Social media can impact the economic well-being of individuals in a number of ways as business owners, employers, employees, and consumers. The example of M-Maji is about economic as well as physical well-being, especially because one of the project's stated goals was to prompt a decrease in water prices through better information about water supply.

Individual economic well-being can benefit very directly from crowdfunding. As a concept, crowdfunding predates the internet—one cannot get less virtual than a fireman standing at an intersection and holding his boot out for donations for charity from passing vehicles—but took on a whole new complexion with the advent of platforms like Kickstarter, Indiegogo, GoFundMe, and Kiva. While there is disagreement, the term appears to date to 2006 and refers to "the raising of funds through the collection of small contributions from the general public (known as the crowd) using the Internet and social media." Though frequently associated with fundraising by entrepreneurial artists, musicians, and independent filmmakers, early successful uses of crowdfunding include President Obama's 2008 election campaign and disaster relief following Hurricane Katrina (Nordicity 2012, 4–5).

Kickstarter is a crowdfunding platform that emphasizes the creative arts, while "Indiegogo was born to empower people to fund what matters to them" (Indiegogo: About Us) and includes campaigns to raise money for entrepreneurial ventures, to protect animals, to purchase health equipment for clinics in developing countries, and to support student organizations, among other categories. GoFundMe focuses on personal causes, allowing campaigns to raise funds for individuals needing medical treatment, remodeling homes to be handicapped accessible, families of people killed in accidents, college tuition for disadvantaged students, and so forth. One recent successful GoFundMe campaign raised over $50,000 as a thank you gift and wedding present for Jon Meis, the Seattle Pacific University building monitor who disarmed the school shooter responsible for killing one and wounding three on June 5, 2014 (GoFundMe: Success Stories 2014).

Kiva takes a slightly different approach to crowdfunding; rather than asking users to donate or contribute to campaigns (charitable or not), it is the "first online lending platform connecting online lenders to entrepreneurs" through microfinance institutions (Kiva: About Us, 2014). Users can lend in increments of $25 to individuals and groups, particularly the poor and underserved, throughout the world—and when the loan is repaid, they can relend or cash out the funds. Loans contribute to funding education, providing agricultural supplies to farmers, or expanding small businesses of many types.

Social media is often considered vital to the economic success of small businesses and their owners. They serve as low-cost or free tools for small business owners who can use them for advertising, to connect with customers and suppliers, and to seek advice on running their businesses. The global economic downturn beginning in 2008 coincided with the creation, increasing awareness, and business utilization of a variety of social media platforms in the United States. "With minimal marketing budgets available to many small businesses, social networking sites offer a quick and, more importantly, free means of promoting their wares to a global audience." For some small businesses, it is a combination of budget and customer base that drives their social media use—some businesses or business locations, such as college towns, rely on tech-savvy customers and must meet their customer needs via social media to survive (Prentice 2009).

Claire Prentice of BBC New York reports on the use of social media by a small cupcake bakery in Washington, D.C., whose owner states that her uses of Facebook and Twitter are vital to the bakery's success: "Together they work like a virtual focus group, a bulletin board, a marketing campaign and branding exercise rolled into one" (2009). Other examples include social media use by small businesses to allow customers to vote on product choices, using the immediacy of Twitter to quickly replace clients who've canceled appointments on short notice, and users soliciting advice from other small business owners on computer software choices. Disadvantages exist, however; Prentice quotes a professor of business who warns that social media is "a conversation rather than an advertising space," that distributing information via social media can overwhelm rather than simply inform customers, and that social media is as much platforms for dissatisfied customers as businesses (Prentice 2009).

In many U.S. cities, the gourmet food truck industry has boomed, increasing its sales and garnering loyal customers by announcing truck locations and specials via social media such as Twitter and Facebook. Roy

Choi, owner of the Kogi Korean taco truck in Los Angeles, initially relied on Twitter because without it he "could have made these tacos, but I would have had no one to sell them to" (Bergman 2009). Today, Kogi uses multiple platforms for multiple purposes: "WordPress for blogging, Twitter for scheduling/emergencies, Facebook for running a temperature check and just interacting with beautiful strangers" (Sniderman 2011). While social media advertising is crucial for Choi's food truck business, it is not without its downsides. His 87,000 followers on Twitter have at times been distracted by "one Kogi dissident (who) created an imposter Twitter account promoting fake events like taco bikini Saturday, and fake dishes like solar-cooked pork, cooked on the roof of the truck. Worse, they lured people to fake locations" (Bergman 2009; Sniderman 2011). Despite the potential downsides, effective use of social media by all types of small businesses benefits the economic well-being of owners, employees, and customers.

For those not self-employed, economic well-being means the ability to find work. LinkedIn had 300 million users worldwide by mid-2014 (LinkedIn: About Us) and is recognized as the number one online social networking site for business professionals. It allows members to create professional profiles, network, and search for jobs (posted on the site by hiring businesses), and even apply for jobs using their LinkedIn profile as a resume through the "Apply with LinkedIn" feature. In 2013, 77 percent of employers were recruiting via social media, and of them 94 percent were using LinkedIn. Employers use LinkedIn's "talent solutions products" to track hiring trends, track employee migration, search member profiles, and directly contact potential recruits (Halzack 2013). As Erika Anderson (2012) of Forbes.com points out, "even in this era, almost 50 percent of people say they got their job through personal connections and networking. LinkedIn allows for personal connection at a distance."

While LinkedIn profiles can help employers and potential employees alike, it's not the only place prospective employers look when investigating potential employees—and careless accounts on other social media platforms can harm one's chances for employment. Nearly half of the human resource managers of the 400 companies surveyed in 2013 by the London-based Institute for Employment Studies said they reviewed potential hires' social media presence during the job search process. While it's been proven true time and again that the unflattering pictures and comments posted on one's social media accounts can hurt one's job prospects, it's interesting to note that a recent study by North Carolina State researchers found job candidates who had been told their social media profiles had been reviewed as part of the candidate-vetting process were less likely to feel the hiring process was fair and more likely to sue, regardless of whether a job offer was made (Jacobson 2014).

Economic well-being means more than just increasing income and finding employment; it also refers to the ability to make economically sound decisions. Sponsored tweets and fake marketing content take advantage of social media's "gray zone," a place where information *presented* as genuine can be incorrectly construed as such by consumers who aren't savvy to social media sponsorship techniques, thereby detracting their ability to make sound decisions. In some cases, such as sponsored tweets, the follower may not realize the celebrity he or she is following is being paid to tweet the brand of shoes she's wearing. For example, Khloe Kardashian is paid $13,000, or $92.86 per character based on Twitter's 140-character limit, every time she tweets about a product to one of her 8.9 million followers. This is according to sponsoredtweets.com, a company that facilitates social media-sponsored campaigns by connecting bloggers, tweeters, and other social media platform users with companies that have products or services they'd like promoted (Sponsoredtweets.com). Until 2011 Twitter endorsements could be made without disclosing that the tweeter had been compensated; however, current Federal Trade Commission (FTC) guidelines require disclosure "when there exists a connection between the endorser and the seller of the advertised product which might materially affect the weight or credibility of the endorsement (that is, the connection is not reasonably expected by the audience) such connection must be fully disclosed" (FTC 2009). In meeting the FTC's guidelines, all sponsored tweets are required to include information identifying them as paid, as are bloggers and other word-of-mouth marketers; however, no standard for doing so exists, leaving it to users to sift through sophisticated marketing techniques to determine the credibility of the information available.

Astroturfing is a social media marketing ploy intended to mislead consumers and unduly influence their spending habits. An example of astroturfing is the writing of fake reviews. In 2013, the New York Attorney General's office announced that "19 companies had agreed to cease their practice of writing fake online reviews for businesses and to pay more than $350,000 in penalties." These search engine optimization companies had been hiring people to write fake reviews for sites like Google Maps, Yelp, and CitySearch by creating fake profiles and using multiple IP addresses to avoid discovery by these sites' fraud detection software. They'd even recruited for this practice by posting job listings on Craigslist.com, Freelancer.com, and oDesk.com. One ad read: "*Hello. . . . We need someone to post 1–2 reviews daily on sites like: Yelp, Google reviews, Citysearch and any other similar sites. We will supply the text/review. You must be able to post these without getting flagged. This will be a long term assignment that will last at least 3 months. We are offering $1.00 dollar for every post. Thank you*" (Schneiderman 2013).

Social media use is thus a double-edged sword when it comes to employment and sound financial decision making. Crowdfunding serves as a further example of the negatives as well as positives. It clearly helps those with successful campaigns, particularly individuals in need, but criticisms abound about ways in which investors, entrepreneurs, and even the economy as a whole can lose. Contributors are not true investors; they may receive rewards for contributing, but they do not receive a share of the profits, do not have any input into the product, and cannot add value to the project. Crowdfunding allows far more projects to find investors than can actually make money, hurting entrepreneurs in the long run—and sometimes projects are simply "crazy ideas" that strike the fancy of a group of contributors but will never sell. Contributors to the highly successful Kickstarter campaign raising more than $5 million for the *Veronica Mars* movie were ridiculed in the press for contributing to the (studio-backed) film rather than to charitable causes; the backers (as Kickstarter donors are called) responded with blogs, tweets, and posts making clear that while they were investing their entertainment dollars they were still contributing to charity (Dupree; Lawson 2013; Mitovich 2013). Whether it's sponsored tweets, fake reviews, small business promotion, or charitable donations, there are political regulations governing those behaviors, which is why economic well-being is also tied to political well-being.

Political Well-Being

The value of social media in politics is controversial and not yet fully researched.

Facebook and Twitter have been credited—and discredited—for the 2011 "Arab Spring" uprisings in the Middle East. Individual political leaders as disparate as U.S. president Barack Obama and Iranian president Hassan Rouhani have Twitter accounts, and NBC's Ann Curry filmed a 2014 documentary "#TwitterDiplomacy" arguing that their tweets to each other, along with other high-level negotiations, helped defuse tensions over Iran's nuclear program. Social media have been declared revolutionary tools for use in politics and political activism and have been decried for promoting "slacktivism" rather than real engagement and participation. Slacktivism is a slang term referring to political activities, such as clicking Facebook's "Like" button regarding political or social issues, that have "no impact on real-life political outcomes, but only serve to increase the feel-good factor of the participants" (Christensen 2011).

Research into how big a change social media represent in politics and political activism, then, is relatively new and ongoing—and the results sometimes contradictory. We can, nevertheless, consider the role of social media in political well-being, although we must also recognize that "political well-being" is not a common term and is also under-researched. Generally, politics is seen as a factor contributing to (or detracting from) individual or societal well-being, rather than political well-being being a subject in and of itself. "The ethical issue of how individuals may live a better or happier life has been discussed and explicitly linked to questions of politics and good government at least since Aristotle's time," with Bentham, Paine, and Malthus also writing on this topic (Duncan 2005, 17). Thus, many definitions of well-being include factors to account for how the politics of a country and community affect individual well-being, especially individual rights and freedoms and political participation.

Human Rights

Human rights, as enshrined by the Universal Declaration of Human Rights, are generally agreed upon individual rights and freedoms necessary not only to life but also to a life of dignity. Certainly abuses of human rights remain far too frequent, and social media have become tools for information dissemination, awareness raising, and action with regard to policies and abuses. Well-known non-governmental human rights organizations such as Amnesty International and Human Rights Watch have Twitter accounts with over 1 million followers each, allowing individual followers to access information about human rights abuses worldwide as well as the organizations' efforts to alleviate them, including calls to action. The United Nations High Commissioner for Refugees disseminates information through its social media presence on Facebook, Twitter, Instagram, Flickr, Pintrest, and YouTube. Government agencies such as the U.S. State Department and scholarly centers such as the United Kingdom's University of Essex Human Rights Centre use Twitter, Facebook, and other social media to explain policy, announce research, and advertise a wide variety of human rights-related information to interested users.

And individuals, particularly influential individuals, can utilize social media to raise awareness and advocate on behalf of human rights. For example, *New York Times* journalist Nicholas Kristof, with nearly 1.5 million Twitter followers, engaged in an awareness and advocacy campaign on behalf of the Rohingya people while traveling in Myanmar (also known as Burma) in spring 2014. The Rohingya are an ethnic group in Myanmar that has suffered human rights abuses for years as a minority of primarily Muslim practitioners among the country's Buddhist majority. Kristof also published a *New York Times* column on the topic (Kristof 2014c), but first utilized his Twitter account to raise awareness and directly advocate U.S. president Obama. This included a tweet with a picture of two emaciated boys and the message: "Malnourished kids in a camp where Burma forcibly confines Rohingya Muslims. Hunger would be worse w/o WFP & ACF." and similar tweets. A couple days later, Kristof moved from awareness to advocacy, tweeting "A petition calling on the White House to pressure Burma to end apartheid against the Rohingya" with a link to the petition (Kristof 2014a, 2014b).

Video- and photo sharing platforms like YouTube, Pinterest, and Facebook also allow individuals to draw attention to human rights abuses. It is for this reason than Diamond (2012b) calls social media "accountability technology" (10). In their research on the 2009 post-election protests in Iran, Yahyanejad and Gheytanchi (2012) conclude that "thanks to widespread use of social media and mobile phones and the advent of citizen journalism, street-level violations of human rights by Iranian officials could no longer be kept in the dark." Their example is the video of a dying Neda Agha-Soltan, shot by Iranian government-backed militia on June 20, 2009. A nearby protestor captured cell phone footage of the "unarmed young woman being shot down and swiftly bleeding to death on a Tehran street." Within three hours, that video footage was on YouTube and had received thousands of hits—and was later picked up by television news and viewed by millions, either partially on broadcasts or fully on website links (146–47).

Individual citizens can use social media to expose human rights abuses through posting photos to Facebook and videos to YouTube or other social media sites. They may also try to use social media to protect themselves from abuses, by utilizing cell phone cameras to record confrontations with police, military, and government officials, with the expectation that in some instances government forces may be less abusive if they know their actions will be posted to the Internet. As Diamond (2012b) points out,

> enter "human rights abuses" into YouTube's search box and you will get roughly ten-thousand videos showing everything from cotton-growers' working conditions in Uzbekistan, to mining practices in the Philippines, to human-organ harvesting in China, to the persecution of Bahá'ís in Iran.

He follows this with an account of how attention to "a YouTube video of a young woman forced by the police to do squats while naked" led the prime minister of Malaysia to request an investigation into police brutality (10).

Social media as tools for awareness and advocacy in the fight for human rights can, unfortunately, be offset by their use to abuse human rights. Authoritarian governments such as China and Iran not only censor information and communication technologies, but also use the same social media tools as protestors of their governments do—but to different ends. Diamond (2012a) calls information and communication technologies (ICTs) "repression-enablers" when they are used by repressive governments to their own ends, such as when "state security mine online photographs and films, heighten Internet filtering and surveillance, and even use ICTs proactively to track down and arrest protest leaders." He concludes that "the balance of potency between ICTs as democracy-boosters and ICTs as repression-enablers remain dynamic and fluid" (xiii).

Political Participation

For an individual to be living well, at least in developed democracies, includes having civil and political rights, one of which is the opportunity to participate politically. Generally, political participation includes activities such as voting, volunteering, awareness and advocacy, fundraising, and protesting. Participation can center on formal elections and political parties, informal political and social movements, and policy issues.

When individual users—citizens—choose to friend, follow, or otherwise access via social media political parties, political organizations, humanitarian organizations, governments, and influential individuals, they often do so for information that will raise their awareness of the issues, policies, and controversies important to them politically and/or to show their support for the organization. In the United States, both major political parties have a presence on Facebook and Twitter, as do less formal ultra-conservative Tea Party organizations. Politically oriented think tanks like the Heritage Foundation, CATO Institute, Council on Foreign Relations, and Brookings Institute all have social media presences as do not-for-profit and humanitarian organizations and movements, such as Sierra Club, American Conservative Union Foundation, and the Half the Sky Movement.

Barack Obama as U.S. president and his administration as the White House have a strong social media presence. Both Barack Obama election campaigns (2008 and 2012) made sophisticated and unprecedented use of the Internet and social media, and his administration continues to do so for important policy issues. Throughout the late 2013/early 2014 push for Americans to sign up for health care under the Affordable Care Act, Twitter followers of President Obama, First Lady Michelle Obama, and the White House received constant reminders (tweets and retweets) to register from the Obamas, government officials, celebrities, and average citizens.

Individuals, organizations, and government actors also use social media to advocate for policy, lobby legislative actors, and raise funds. Advocacy and lobbying can be to change or terminate existing policies as well as implement or block proposed policies. Individuals can use social media to advocate for—and against—policy change in democracies and even in non-democracies. Recent examples in the United States include campaigns related to policies regarding the minimum wage, wage equality for women, and marriage equality. Even in China—an authoritarian country with repressive censorship and internet access policies—citizens have effectively used social media for grassroots protests against their government. Xiao (2012) provides the example of a proposed chemical factory in the city of Xiamen in Fujian Province. In 2007, Chinese bloggers posted warnings about the "potentially disastrous" environmental impact of the planned paraxylene factory. Though the government tried to delete posts and messages against the factory, the campaign also spread "via e-mail, instant messages, and text messages on mobile phones." A protest was eventually held outside city hall and thousands of participants utilized cellphones and social media to chronicle the protest online. The government responded by holding public hearings and, six months later, decided against building the plant in Xiamen. Xiao (2012) concludes that "the Xiamen story marks the rise of a remarkable new force in China's contemporary social and political life: popular opinion (communicated online)" (64).

The value of social media in political participation, particularly political activism, remains controversial. Malcolm Gladwell (2010) argues in "Small Change: Why the Revolution Will Not be Tweeted," that "social networks are effective at increasing participation—by lessening the level of motivation that participation requires." He compares the hierarchically organized and successful U.S. civil rights protests of the 1960s with the loosely organized social networks built through social media. He contrasts the high degree of personal connection in the civil rights protests with the "weak ties" built by social media, and argues that weak ties do not a revolution make:

> [social media] makes it easier for activists to express themselves, and harder for that expression to have any impact. The instruments of social media is well suited to making the existing social order more efficient. They are not a natural enemy of the status quo.

Gladwell (2010) has a point, and he further makes it by pointing out that "the Facebook page of the Save Darfur Coalition has 1,282,339 members, who have donated an average of nine cents apiece" to the charity. On Twitter, one can frequently find political tweets that say some version of "retweet if you support X," but what does that retweet actually do? It makes the followers feel good about themselves, perhaps, but may go no further. This low-effort, low-impact participation is termed "slacktivism."

At the same time, however, participation *could* go further: savvy Twitter account holders can gather and report statistics such as significantly high numbers of replies and retweets to targeted political organizations or government officials, demonstrating support for an issue or campaign. And some followers may become not only more aware politically but more active as a result of such tweets; low-impact political participation through social media can create a comfort level that allows individuals to take on higher-impact activities, both virtual and face to face.

Although Alterman (2011) agrees that "The Revolution Will Not Be Tweeted," he gives social media more credit than Gladwell (2010). In reviewing the use of media in the Arab uprisings of 2011, specifically Tunisia and Egypt, Alterman concludes "It was not Twitter and Facebook, but television that was absolutely fundamental to the unfolding of events." However, he points out that much of the content reported on television would not have existed but for social media—and that "social media and user-generated content lowered the threshold to become an activist, making it easier for people to see themselves as activists within a movement" (103, 112).

Social media can thus contribute to political situations affecting individual well-being as well as detract from it. Activists have used cellphones and social media to inform and motivate, just as governments have used it to punish those motivated to protest and opposition. It is a set of tools that can bring the needless death of one woman to the attention of millions, or can dissipate the will to act into little more than a willingness to "click." We remain too early in the use of the tools to know whether social media will "reinvent social activism" or "if what happens next is more of the same" (Gladwell 2010).

CONCLUSION

There are far more varied ways for social media use to help or harm individual well-being than there are ways to say so. They are new and still rapidly changing technologies, so conclusions about their uses and influence on well-being are challenging to draw and are often quickly outdated. There are, hopefully, more ways social media is used to help rather than harm physical and economic well-being, such as M-Maji or food truck tweets. Social media use detracting from physical and emotional well-being, however, receive far more attention, as Craigslist killers and cyberbullied suicides make headlines. The impact of social media on political well-being remains oft-debated but fascinating as democracies and authoritarian regimes alike react to the technologies and their citizens' use of them for political participation. Social media's impact on social well-being is perhaps most complex, as to an extent it incorporates all of the above as well as its uses for our social lives.

It is, ultimately, individuals who choose to use social media as tools for extreme or balanced behavior. The individual challenges to using social media ethically and to contribute to individual well-being are as numerous today as when Aristotle's first suggested his idea that "flourishing" requires individuals to "exercise 'practical reason'" (Patterson and Wilkins 2008, 8). Social media represent considerable change in mediated communication, but remain, "in the end . . . merely a tool, open to both noble and nefarious purposes" (Diamond 2012b, 5).

REFERENCES

Alterman, J. B. (2011). "The Revolution will not be Tweeted." *The Washington Quarterly*, 34: 4, 103–116 doi: 10.1080/0163660X.2011.610714.

Anderson, E. (2012). "Top 2 Reasons LinkedIn is Taking Over the World." *Forbes*. Retrieved July 8, 2014 from www.forbes.com/sites/erikaandersen/2012/05/11/top-2-reasons-linkedin-is-taking-over-the-world/.

AshleyMadison.com.

Beasley, B. (2013). "Introduction." In *Social media and the value of truth*, eds. B. Beasley and M. Haney. Lanham, MD: Lexington Books. 1–2.

Bell, P. (2014). "People Who Self-Harm Will Do So Anyway: A Report on the Role of Social Media in Self-Harming." Retrieved June 30, 2014 from www.huffingtonpost.co.uk/2014/01/29/self-harm-social-media-report_n_4687261.html.

Bennett, S. (2013, June 18). "One in Four People Worldwide Use Social Media." Retrieved July 10, 2014 from www.mediabistro.com/alltwitter/social-media-worldwide-growth_b45043.

Bergman, B. (2009). "Tweeting Food Truck Draws L.A.'s Hungry Crowds." *National Public Radio*. Retrieved March 15, 2014 from www.npr.org/templates/story/story.php?storyId=101881984.

Chhabra, E. (2013). "Ubiquitous across Globe, Cellphones Have Become Tool for Doing Good." *New York Times*. Retrieved March 14, 2014 from www.nytimes.com/2013/11/08/giving/ubiquitous-across-globe-cellphones-have-become-tool-for-doing-good.html?_r=0.

Christensen, H. S. (2011). "Political Activities on the Internet: Slacktivism or Political Participation by Other Means?" *First Monday*, vol. 16, 2–7. Retrieved July 11, 2014, from firstmonday.org/ojs/index.php/fm/rt/printerFriendly/3336/2767.

Crisp, R. (2013). "Well-Being." *The Stanford Encyclopedia of Philosophy*, ed. Edward N. Zalta. Retrieved February 6, 2014 from plato.stanford.edu/entries/well-being/.

Diamond, L. (2012a). "Introduction." In *Liberation Technology: Social Media and the Struggle for Democracy*, eds. L. Diamond and M. Plattner. Baltimore: The Johns Hopkins University Press. ix–xxvii.

Diamond, L. (2012b). "Liberation Technology." In *Liberation Technology: Social Media and the Struggle for Democracy*, eds. L. Diamond and M. Plattner. Baltimore: The Johns Hopkins University Press. 3–17.

Dupree, S. (n.d.) "Crowdfunding 101: Pros and Cons." Retrieved July 6, 2014 from www.gsb.stanford.edu/ces/crowdfunding-101.

Duncan, G. (2005). "What do we mean by 'happiness'? The Relevance of Subjective Wellbeing to Social Policy." *Social Policy Journal of New Zealand*, 25, 16–31.

Englander, E. (2012). "Digital Self-Harm: Frequency, Type, Motivations, and Outcomes." Retrieved July 7, 2014 from webhost.bridgew.edu/marc/DIGITAL%20SELF%20HARM%20report.pdf.

Fletcher, G. (2013). "A Fresh Start for the Objective-Live Theory of Well-Being." *Utilitas* 25, 206–220. doi: 10.1017/S0953820812000453.

Federal Trade Commission. (2009, October 5). "FTC Publishes Final Guides Governing Endorsements, Testimonials." Retrieved July 7, 2014 from www.ftc.gov/news-events/press-releases/2009/10/ftc-publishes-final-guides-governing-endorsements-testimonials.

Gladwell, M. (2010, October 4). "Small Change: Why the Revolution will not be Tweeted." *The New Yorker*. Retrieved April 9, 2014 from www.newyorker.com/reporting/2010/10/04/101004fa_fact_gladwell?currentPage=all.

GoFundMe: Success Stories (2014). Retrieved July 6, 2014 from www.gofundme.com/success.

Grandoni, D. (2014, June 29). "You May Have Been a Lab Rat in a Huge Facebook Experiment." Retrieved July 7, 2014 from www.huffingtonpost.com/2014/06/29/facebook-experiment-psychological_n_5540018.html.

Gummow, J. (2014, April 24). "8 Ways to have a Relationship in the Digital Age without Going Insane." Retrieved July 7, 2014 from www.alternet.org/culture/8-ways-have-relationship-digital-age-without-going-insane.

Halzack, S. (2013). "LinkedIn has Changed the Way Businesses Hunt Talent." *Washington Post.* Retrieved July 8, 2014 from www.washingtonpost.com/business/capitalbusiness/linkedin-has-changed-the-way-businesses-hunt-talent/2013/08/04/3470860e-e269-11e2-aef3-339619eab080_story.html.

Indiegogo: About US. (2014). Retrieved July 6, 2014 from www.indiegogo.com/about/our-story?gclid=CMKO1rHptr8CFZRj7AodyzQAfw.

Jacobson, R. (2014, January 13). "Facebook Snooping on Job Candidates may Backfire for Employers." *Scientific American.* Retrieved July 8, 2014 from www.scientificamerican.com/article/facebook-snooping-on-job/.

Kaplan, A. M., and M. Haenlein. (2010) "Users of the World, Unite! The Challenges and Opportunities of Social Media." *Business Horizons,* 53, 59–68.

Konnikova, M. (2013, September 10). "How Facebook Makes Us Unhappy." *The New Yorker.* Retrieved July 10, 2014 from www.newyorker.com/online/blogs/elements/2013/the-real-reason-facebook-makes-us-unhappy.html?printable=true&currentPage=all.

Krikorian, R. (2013). "New Tweets Per Second Record, and How!" *Engineering Blog.* Retrieved March 14, 2014 from blog.twitter.com/2013/new-tweets-per-second-record-and-how.

Kristof, N. [Nicholas Kristof]. (2014a, May 27). "Malnourished Kids in a Camp Where Burma Forcibly Confines Rohingya Muslims. Hunger would be Worse w/o WFP & ACF." pic.twitter.com/XRbGi9kfmC [Tweet]. Retrieved from twitter.com/Nick-Kristof/status/471402990491164672.

Kristof, N. [Nicholas Kristof]. (2014b, May 29). "A Petition Calling on the White House to Pressure Burma to end Apartheid Against the Rohingya: petitions.whitehouse.gov/petition/pressure-burmese-government-end-abuses-against-rohingya-and-other-ethnic-minorities/hDmrz4xB" [Tweet]. Retrieved from htwitter.com/NickKristof/status/472096697850822656.

Kristof, N. (2014c, June 1). "Obama Success or Global Shame." *New York Times.* Retrieved on June 1, 2014 from www.nytimes.com/2014/06/01/opinion/sunday/kristof-obama-success-or-global-shame.html?_r=0.

Kurtzlben, D. (2014). "How Twitter's User Growth Compares to Facebook's." *US News & World Report.* Retrieved March 15, 2014 from www.usnews.com/news/blogs/datamine/2014/02/06/how-twitters-user-growth-compares-to-facebooks.

Lawson, R. (2013, March 13). "Anybody know of a better charity than the 'Veronica Mars' movie?" *The Wire.* Retrieved July 6, 2014 from www.thewire.com/entertainment/2013/03/kickstarter-kind-of-annoying-isnt-it/63060/.

LinkedIn: About Us. (2014). Retrieved July 8, 2014 from www.linkedin.com/about-us?trk=hb_ft_about.

Love is Louder The Movement. Retrieved March 15, 2014 from www.loveislouder.com/the-movement/.

Lysiak, M. (2014, April 28). "Exclusive: Craigslist Killer Miranda Barbour Tells How and Why She Killed." *Newsweek.* Retrieved June 27 2014 from www.newsweek.com/2014/05/09/exclusive-craigslist-killer-miranda-barbour-tells-how-and-why-she-killed-248670.html.

McPhee, M. (2010, August 16). "Craigslist Killer Philip Markoff Wrote Ex-Fiancée's Name in Blood as He Killed Himself." *ABC News.* Retrieved June 27, 2014 from abcnews.go.com/US/TheLaw/craigslist-killer-philip-markoff-swallowed-toilet-paper-revived/story?id=11413302.

Mitovich, M. W. (2013). "The *Veronica Mars* Movie Kickstarter Campaign: Don't You Dare Feel Bad about Chipping In." *TVLine.com.* Retrieved July 6, 2014 from tvline.com/2013/03/14/veronica-mars-movie-kickstarter/.

"M-Maji" (2014). Retrieved on March 14, 2014 from mmaji.wordpress.com/m-maji/.

"National Wellbeing Wheel of Measures." (2013). UK Office of National Statistics. Retrieved February 6, 2014 from www.ons.gov.uk/well-being.

Neufeldt, V., and D. B. Guralnik. (Eds.). (1991). *Webster's New world Dictionary of American English, Third College Edition*. Cleveland, OH: Webster's New World.

Nordicity. (2012) "Crowdfunding in a Canadian Context: Exploring the Potential of Crowdfunding in the Creative Content Industries." Retrieved July 8, 2014 from www.cmf-fmc.ca/documents/files/about/publications/CMF-Crowdfunding-Study.pdf.

Nussbaum, M. (2006). *Frontiers of Justice: Disability, Nationality, Species Membership*. Cambridge, MA: Harvard University Press.

"Parents: Cyber Bullying Led to Teen's Suicide." (2007, November 19). *ABC News*. Retrieved June 30, 2014 from abcnews.go.com/GMA/story?id=3882520.

Patterson, P., and L. Wilkins. (2008). *Media Ethics: Issues & Cases, Sixth Edition*. Boston: McGraw Hill Higher Education.

Perez Jr., J. (2014, May 1). "East Chicago Police Offer Up Their Lobby, Parking Lot for Craigslist Transactions." *Chicago Tribune*. Retrieved June 30, 2014 from articles.chicagotribune.com/2014-05-01/news/chi-east-chicago-police-offer-up-their-lobby-parking-lot-for-craigslist-transactions-20140501_1_craigslist-transactions-becker-lobby.

Prentice, C. (2009). "Twitter and Facebook Aid Small Firms." Retrieved March 15, 2014 from news.bbc.co.uk/2/hi/business/8273667.stm.

Qizilbash, M. (2013). "On Capability and the Good Life: Theoretical Debates and their Practical Implications." *Philosophy & Public Policy Quarterly* 31: 2, 35–42.

Reno Street Food. (2014). Retrieved March 16, 2014 from www.facebook.com/RenoStreetFood.

Robeyns, I. (2011). "The Capability Approach." *The Stanford Encyclopedia of Philosophy*, ed. Edward N. Zalta. Retrieved March 6, 2014 from plato.stanford.edu/entries/capability-approach/.

Rodriguez, M. (2014, March 11). "Mother, Daughter Separated by War Reunited in Denver." Retrieved July 7, 2014 from www.9news.com/story/news/local/2014/03/12/mother-daughter-separated-by-war-in-south-sudan-reunited-in-denver/6311409/.

Sankin, A. (2014, May 6). "Mapping 30 Days of Craigslist Crimes." *Dailydot.com*. Retrieved July 7, 2014, from dailydot.com/crime/craigslist-crime-map/.

Schorr, M. (2013, November 17). "The State of Extramarital Affairs." *Boston Globe*. Retrieved July 7, 2014 from www.bostonglobe.com/magazine/2013/11/17/the-state-extramarital-affairs-getting-caught-and-cheater-meter/o3juJzkgQwkJ6GOu0bXliO/story.html.

Schneiderman, E. (2013, July 7). "A. G. Schneiderman Announces Agreement with 19 Companies to Stop Writing Fake Online Reviews and Pay More Than $350,000 in Fines." Retrieved July 7, 2014 from www.ag.ny.gov/press-release/ag-schneiderman-announces-agreement-19-companies-stop-writing-fake-online-reviews.

Seavert, L. (2012). "Teen Creates Viral Campaign to Stop Cyberbullies." *USA Today*. Retrieved March 15, 2014 from usatoday30.usatoday.com/news/health/wellness/story/2012-08-17/teen-twitter-cyberbullies/57120166/1.

Sniderman, Z. (2011). "How Social Media is Fueling the Food Truck Phenomenon." *Mashable.com*. Retrieved March 15, 2014 from mashable.com/2011/06/16/food-trucks-social-media/.

Social Progress Imperative: Social Progress Index. (2013). Retrieved February 6, 2014 from www.socialprogressimperative.org/data/spi.

Sparks Food Truck Drive-In. (2014). Retrieved March 16, 2014 from www.facebook.com/foodtruckdrivein.

Stanglin D. and W. M. Welch. (2013, October 16). "Two Girls Arrested on Bullying Charges after Suicide." *USA Today*. Retrieved June 30, 2014 from www.usatoday.com/story/news/nation/2013/10/15/florida-bullying-arrest-lakeland-suicide/2986079/.

State of the Media: Social Media Report 2012. (2012). Retrieved March 14, 2014 from www.nielsen.com/us/en/newswire/2012/social-media-report-2012-social-media-comes-of-age.html.

The Jed Foundation: History. Retrieved March 15, 2014 from www.jedfoundation.org/about/history.

Twitter Usage. (2014, June 25). Retrieved June 30, 2014 from: about.twitter.com/company.

Walker, A. J. (2014, June 18). "Suspected Craigslist Killer's Bond Upped to $1.5M." Retrieved June 30, 2014 from wtnh.com/2014/06/18/craigslist-killer-in-court/.

Wellbeing Concepts (n.d.). U.S. Centers for Disease Control. Retrieved February 6, 2014 from www.cdc.gov/hrqol/wellbeing.htm.

Williams, R. (2014, June 25). "World Cup Boosts Tinder Use in Brazil by 50pc." *The Telegraph.* Retrieved July 8, 2014 from www.telegraph.co.uk/technology/news/10924623/World-Cup-boosts-Tinder-use-in-Brazil-by-50pc.html.

Winterman, D. (2013). "Cyber Self-Harm: Why Do People Troll Themselves Online?" *BBC News Magazine.* Retrieved December 4, 2013 from www.bbc.com/news/magazine-25120783.

Xiao, Q. (2012). "The Battle for the Chinese Internet." In *Liberation Technology: Social Media and the Struggle for Democracy,* eds. L. Diamond and M. Plattner. Baltimore: The Johns Hopkins University Press. 63–77.

Yahyanejad, M., and E. Gheytanchi. (2012). "Social Media, Dissent, and Iran's Green Movement." In *Liberation Technology: Social Media and the Struggle for Democracy,* eds. L. Diamond and M. Plattner. Baltimore: The Johns Hopkins University Press. 139–153.

II

Social Media's Influence on a Society's Well-Being

SIX

The Community of Sanity in the Age of the Meme[1]

Mitchell R. Haney

The spread of the use of social media within less than a decade has been colossal. As of January 2014, Facebook alone had over a billion active users (and over 700 million daily users). And Facebook was a month shy of being ten years old. And it is only one of numerous social media platforms. Much like the spread of other communications technology of the past, the telephone, television, and so on, social media has an impact on how people connect with each other and how they transmit meaning among each other. A very popular use of social media has become the transmission of the Internet meme. These are images, text, or a combination of the two, aimed at communicating a succinct and usually prescriptive message to other users in one's network. And those that people find catchy in some way are shared and spread across the social media outlets. Internet memes are the electronic analog of what bumper stickers or t-shirts have been for at least four decades.

The aim of this chapter is to raise two ethical concerns about the use of Internet memes and their potential effects on the well-being of society. These may be concerns that are true of bumper stickers or t-shirts as well, but whose nature in the relative culture of social media may be more pernicious. In the milieu of viral spread of information and ideas of the Internet there are two concerns: a) Many memes promote types of reasoning which are not conducive to reasonable discussion of important issues in our pluralistic society; b) Many memes vilify the Other in a way that communicates that they are so different and so bad that they ought to be ignored or ostracized.

THE INTERNET MEME: A BRIEF SURVEY

The term "meme" was first introduced by Richard Dawkins in *The Selfish Gene* (1976). He coined the term as a way of trying to identify how ideas, behaviors, styles, and so on within culture are reproduced from person to person, and across the community. As an evolutionary biologist, Dawkins was thinking that cultural units of meaning may be selected and transmitted through a culture in a way that is similar to the transmission of genes. Those meanings that take hold as meaningful, for example, practically, socially, philosophically, and so on, will be transmitted and reproduced. Those meanings that fail to take hold in the minds of members of the culture will be weeded out, not reproduced, and in some sense go extinct.

In the age of the Internet, we have what is now referred to as the "Internet meme." For most people participating in social media, they are just called "memes"; not knowing that it originally referred to the cultural transmission of meanings generally. The Internet meme, as was stated above, typically takes a photograph or a simply a blank canvas and adds some short meaningful message. The creator posts the meme he or she creates to a social media platform or in a meme generator service (or both), and those that like the meme will share it in their social media networks, and so on and so on. Thus, successful memes will transmit across the culture of the Internet and social media. Those that are really successful will take hold as cultural references outside of the realm of social media and the Internet. Unsuccessful memes will die off from lack of reproduction.

Internet memes have become so popular in the realm of social media that a number of popular websites are dedicated to helping users create their own memes. These include memegenerator.com and knowyourmeme.com. Within these websites you will finds thousands upon thousands of memes created by people from around the globe. Many use images and play on phrases already in cultural memory. For instance, the image of Boromir, from Peter Jackson's film of *The Fellowship of the Ring* (2001), where he proclaims, "One does not simply walk into Mordor!" is very popular for memetic play. Figure 6.1 is an example of meme creation done on memegenerator.com

There is a large selection of images one can use, many of which are as popular or more popular than Boromir. There are those that are popular simply because of social media. There are the likes of Annoying Facebook Girl, Angry Cat, Trollface, Bad Luck Brian, and others that have been or remain ubiquitous in social media. One can also simply create memes with phrases on a background. No one is limited to just using these websites, one can create them with a number of different graphics and word processor software programs.

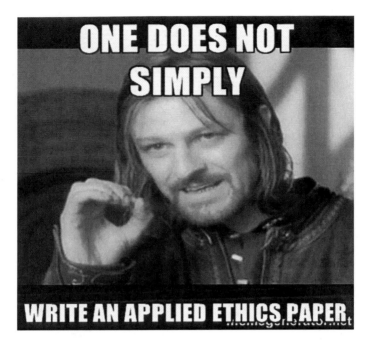

Figure 6.1.

The aim of memes can be various. They can attempt to convey a serious message concerning some element of human life that the creator and those who share it want to express. Typically the serious memes are expressive of some ethical or political prescription, or support of some public message, which those creating or sharing want to impress upon others. They can also be meant to convey humor or just an emotion. Or they can try to mix any of these.

For instance, figure 6.2 conveys what the sharer feels is a public service message (from Hellopeter.com on Facebook). It conveys a warning to beware of new ways in which criminals may gain access to one's bank account.

Figure 6.3 is an example of something done with the aim of making people laugh (from memegenerator.com). It takes a popular "low culture" phrase and juxtaposes it to an image of "high-culture" for humorous effect.

There is nothing ethically problematic about the use of memes for either of these types of activities. The former works almost like a newspaper headline in grabbing people's attention for the purpose of conveying a piece of news that the creator or those who share it believe it will serve the public interest. The second may be simply good, because a life devoid of humor may not be worth living. However, not all memes are

Figure 6.2.

helpful or good. Many memes, I will argue, may have a pernicious effect on goods we want to see flourish in the public realm and for the common good.

MEMES AND THE COMMUNITY OF SANITY

The Community of Sanity

The philosopher Hilary Putnam in "Why is a Philosopher?" (1990) argues that,

> What is better or worse to say about most questions of real human concern is not just a matter of *opinion*. Recognizing that this is so is the essential price of admission to the community of sanity. (114)

According to Putnam, to have a functioning moral community, that is, a community of people trying to get along in morally appropriate ways, it must be held that there are better and worse reasons for various positions on ethical and political topics. A failure to hold that will succumb to might makes right or the tyranny of the majority. Members of the community sanity ought to hold that there are better and worse answers to those moral and political questions which aid in the community in flour-

Figure 6.3.

ishing in living together. What are necessary assumptions, in an abstract way, for holding that there are better or worse things to say on important questions includes that members of the community of sanity abide by certain standards of reasoning and comportment. These standards may include:

1. Acknowledgment that rightness is a matter of justification.
2. Willingness to muster reasons and consider other's reasons for a position.
3. Humility to accept good criticisms.
4. Engage debate in a cooperative rather than merely combative manner since getting things right is of utmost importance for all affected.

Under Putnam's philosophical position truth, correctness, or rightness are grounded in giving reasons for a claim that is under consideration, and such reasons are able to be put to public scrutiny. Those reasons that are able to survive the standards employed in public scrutiny are better than those reasons that will die under such review. This is nothing entirely new. Plato thought justification is what separated knowledge from merely true belief. This standard of truth or correctness requires that those who want to be members of the community of sanity must give reasons for their claims, and be open to receiving reasons from others. They must also acknowledge that there are standards of what will count as good reasons and what will count as poor reasons, and those standards apply to all who come to the discussion (including him or herself). Finally, those that are genuinely concerned with getting things right rather than just being right will approach debate with a complex attitude of humility, intellectual courage, and cooperation rather than arrogance, intellectual cowardice, and combativeness.

Those members of the wider intellectual community that are concerned with, for instance, logic and evidence, all know that there are some forms of reasoning and use of facts that are simply fallacious. There is a long list of formal and informal fallacies which members of the community hope to avoid and to curtail in others. The fallacies include such things as name calling, confusing correlation with causation, equivocation, and hasty generalization, among many others. The reason members of the community are concerned with using and supporting good reasoning, as well as avoiding bad reasoning, is that they think good reasoning is a necessary condition for establishing the correctness of an assertion, and fallacious reasoning does no such thing. Fallacious reasoning and poor use of evidence, members of the community themselves have reason to believe, establish nothing. A fallacious argument fails to support the correctness of a conclusion. Those in the community of sanity should want a community-wide adherence to standards of good reasoning in order to aim at getting things right about important questions of human concern. Thus, they attempt to role model, educate, and enforce standards for good reasoning with themselves and others.

Memes in the Community of Sanity

As was noted in the beginning, successful memes will spread across the space of social media. They go viral, as is now said about the spread of videos, memes, and so on across the Internet. However, not only does the particular meme go viral, so does the message and the form of reasoning it reflects. What people perceive in the space of social media can impact their psychology, including attitudes and emotions. For those that may be skeptical that social media can impact users, Facebook in 2012 manipulated users' newsfeeds to see whether or not they could impact their emotions and attitudes. They selected more than 600,000 users and without their knowledge manipulated their newsfeeds for one week and recorded their posts for analysis. Some users were shown only negative posts and others only positive posts. Facebook and its research partners reported a statistically significant impact in being able to alter users' emotions and attitudes (positively and negatively) with this manipulation of their feeds (McNeal 2014). Thus, we have evidence that what appears in social media does impact users psychologically.

Given the ubiquitous use of memes and the fact that many are used to prescribe various attitudes about various topics of important human concern, and that they model certain forms of reasoning, we should be concerned about what kinds of attitudes and reasoning are being portrayed in the viral spread of memes. From the point of view of wanting to support good reasoning and curtail poor reasoning in order to maintain a community of sanity, we ought to reflect on this popular form of prescriptive community in a vast and widely utilized medium of social media. However, it seems that many memes undermine the attitudes and habits of reasoning demanded by the standards of good reasoning, and, thus, threaten to undermine the community of sanity in their viral spread.

Let us look to some example memes all found on people's social media pages about hot button issues of important public concern. Consider figure 6.4, a meme about state level welfare programs and the Democratic Party in U.S. politics.

Or consider figure 6.5, that offers a characterization of anti-welfare conservatives.

In both examples, we have memes expressing an attitude about the nature or value of state welfare programs but also an attitude about the people who either support or do not support state welfare programs.

Figure 6.4.

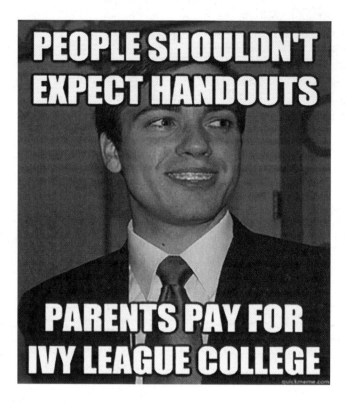

Figure 6.5.

Many memes on important topics not only express attitudes about a specific position, but attitudes and beliefs about those persons sympathetic to the position being criticized. There is something not entirely unique about this. Political cartoons have a long history of not only vilifying positions, but vilifying those who support such positions. In some ways, though, memes are a bit unique. First, political cartoonists sign their name to their work and are publicly responsible for what they say and portray (as are the media outlets that publish their cartoons). Second, political cartoons in traditional media are subject to review prior to publication. Third, political cartoons can be spread as memes do through social media, but they typically appear in mainstream media first. Memes as they are typically created and spread have no authorial responsibility, no editorial oversight, and can be generated and shared in just a few minutes (the creative process is not a drawn out reflective process in most cases). However, notice that in the two memes above, there is a clear set of fallacies which are being utilized and modeled, if the memes catch on, and being successful reproduced in the network of social media (even if as it is with the cases above they are also meant to be humorous).

Each of these memes engages in hasty generalizations (either directly or presumed as a premise). These fallacious claims include: All welfare recipients are lazy. All welfare recipients are Democrats. All those who are against welfare are wealthy. All those against welfare are dependent on inherited wealth and they are lazy as well. Certainly in a discussion or debate over the justification of welfare (or any serious social disagreement), we do not want to spread the idea that we can use hasty generalizations about one's opposition (or even as reasons in support of a policy). Hasty generalizations are fallacious and undermine our ability to get the correct or right position because they assert predicates of all in a class without any substantial evidence for that predication. In addition, some of the generalizations assumed or employed in these memes are flat out name calling. Those with family wealth are spoiled and lazy. Those who receive welfare are lazy and self-serving. These are assumptions communicated via these two memes that essentially just call the opposition bad names. Name calling is clearly among the most fallacious rhetorical ploys in the book (although unfortunately all too effective). Simply calling one's opposition morally pejorative names and one's confederates morally laudatory names has no impact on whether or not what they believe is likely to be correct or rational. The unfortunate truth is that many fallacies, if not most, that are rhetorically effective in moving people to believe things can and will often show up in memes in social media. And we know that social media networks impact human thought if the message is reinforced, and memes can reinforce certain types of reasons and reasoning (as any rhetoric can do) as they go viral across the space of social media.

A significant concern then with the use of Internet memes is not just that certain content may be spread virally but the acceptance of certain intellectual bad habits and attitudes about reasoning and the giving of reasons may spread as acceptable. (With the caveat that it's not just through memes that such reasoning may be culturally spread. All one needs to do is listen to talk radio or watch various talk shows to understand that this is the case. They are rife with use of some of the most basic fallacies as well.) But memes and their use in social media can be a danger to keeping people in the community of sanity which requires we aim at good reasoning and avoid bad reasoning. The influence of memes is, in part, due to the fact that social media can influence in a way similar to peer pressure since the ideas contained in memes are posted by users' "friends." Members of the community of sanity will want to address and curtail the spread of bad forms of reasoning contained in memes as a popular form of communication. Members want to do this for the express purpose that we as a community need to tackle our most pressing social concerns and fallacious reasoning gets us no closer to correct answers but befuddles and taints the pursuit of such.

Memes and the Ostracism of the Other[2]

Another and possibly more pernicious worry about Internet memes and their viral nature of influence is that in many cases they portray people with whom members of the community should engage over pressing moral and social issues, as so wholly other that they are not worth engaging for the betterment of our communal lives. Much in the same way that there was name calling in the examples above, there is a common meme theme of portraying those who differ in their views from us as so utterly alien or perverse that we need not even seek to invite them into the community of sanity. There is an expressed attitude of justifiable exclusion.

Throughout the history of modern ethics, there has been sensitivity to how we treat the Other. Do we show them respect as persons, as individuals, as well as members of the moral general community? One can find this in the work of Immanuel Kant (1956, trans. Paton), as well as those in the existential and phenomenological traditions such as Jean-Paul Sartre (1943) and Emmanuel Levinas (1969). To have a community of individuals that seek to find the correct answers to questions of significant human concern, especially in a pluralistic world, a wide circle must be cast to include people of different attitudes, habits, and beliefs. Members should be tolerant of those that have different attitudes, habits, and beliefs from their own. The community of sanity demands that we be open to the reasoning of others different from ourselves, and give such reasoning due consideration. This does not mean members must accept their reasoning and attitudes in the end, but members should welcome each other's arguments, be open to each other's criticisms, and assess such on the basis of the standards of good reasoning and evidence. However, many memes are used to cast others who disagree out of the community of sanity. Memes are often used to portray the members of the opposition as so wholly other as to not be worthy of an ear.

Consider the portrayals in figures 6.6 and 6.7 of people on opposing sides of the gun control issue in the following memes.

In these two memes, we see a common theme of demeaning members of the opposition as so unworthy of due consideration in the discussion that we ought to cast them out of the community of sanity. We should not take them at all seriously in the pursuit of correct answers (in this case over gun control). We need not listen to "them."

Notice that members of the opposing sides are portrayed as in some sense outside the parameters of who ought to be members of the community of sanity; who are worthy of being part of the discussion of this important issue. In figure 6.6, the image of a slovenly man, distastefully displaying himself with his guns, is used to say that we need gun control because those that are against gun control either are like this man or must be so irrational as to want to protect this man's right to bear arms, that we

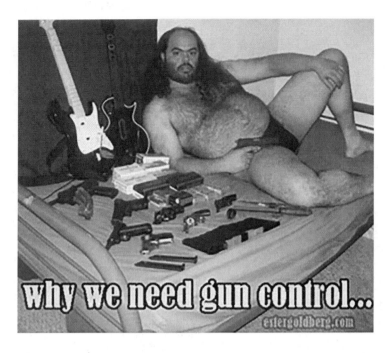

Figure 6.6.

just shouldn't take them at all seriously. In figure 6.7, the image of Willy Wonka is coupled with an often used piece of rhetoric about gun control. It is that gun control only harms law abiding citizens because criminals—almost by definition of the word—flaunt the law. This meme communicates the idea that all those in favor of gun control are childishly naïve. The hidden assumption here is that we don't include children in the community of those who seek answers to pressing issues of moral and social concern because they are too intellectually immature to participate in the community of sanity. Hence, here we have two memes (and there are multitudes of these types of memes on all sorts of pressing moral and social issues), which demonstrate the move to ostracize others as so other, as utterly alien or insufficiently rational, as to not take people of different opinion on a contentious issue with any position but disdain and only worthy of being ignored. Memes such as these send the clear message that members of one side need not entertain the thoughts of those on the other side. Instead, it communicates the belief and attitude that others of different opinion should simply be deported from the community of sanity, and if they are not members, then there is no requirement to listen to them and consider their reasons. This is a cowardly but efficient way to narrow the community of sanity to only like-minded individuals.

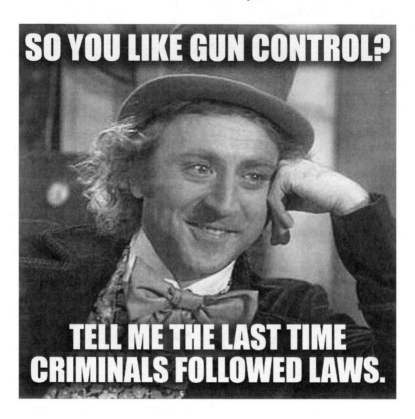

Figure 6.7.

COMMUNAL WELL-BEING, HUMOR, AND RHETORIC

The driving reason for why we should be committed to the standards contained in Putnam's idea of the community of sanity is that obtaining the right answers to issues of deep human concern is that having such answers is in part constitutive of having a flourishing community. Or, at the very least, having a community which has vital and important discussions of such issues is constitutive of a flourishing community. I will not offer here a theory of communal flourishing, but I take it that this value includes such things as: reasonable tolerance of differences, openness to a plurality of beliefs, and cooperation in shared projects (including discussions and decisions of what policies to hold across the community). Granted these standards assume that a pluralistic world is, at least, inescapable or very unlikely to be escaped. The conditions of the community of sanity are part and parcel of what is required for communal flourishing in a pluralistic world.

If communal flourishing requires the standards of the community of sanity be achieved or, at least, there be some vigilance in trying to achieve the standards, then we ought to be concerned with forms of communication and discussion which hinder us in such an achievement. If what was argued above has some plausibility, then we should be concerned about the nature and value of the form of communication in Internet memes. In addition, we ought to think about how best to handle them in the space of social media. But many may not be convinced that there is really much of a worry. Or they may say that the worry is not such a threat as to constitute a need to take any action.

Defenders of the types of memes above may object to my concerns on a number of grounds. First, they may say that those that create and share such memes in the space of social media are exercising their right to freedom of expression and due to this protection ought not be dissuaded from creating and sharing such expressions. And the protection of freedom of expression is also a part of communal flourishing in a pluralistic world. Second, that one should not take these memes too seriously because they are obviously attempts at humor which indicates that the creators and those who share them mean them to be tongue-in-cheek. Third, memes are not more or less pernicious than other places we find the use of effective but fallacious rhetoric. Hence, there is nothing special about the use of memes in social media.

It does not follow from raising concerns and offering critique of some popular form of expression that one ought to prohibit its use. It is true that freedom of expression is one protection that contributes to a flourishing community. As a result, people's right to freedom of expression ought to be protected (except in the typical limit cases of clear and present danger of harm to others). However, as J. S. Mill argued in *On Liberty*, even if we allow people the liberty to do as they wish, it doesn't follow that we cannot engage in moral approbation and disapprobation. Thus, the concerns raised here are engaging in the moral evaluation of the particular form of expression, and doing so even if everyone has a right to express what they desire.

Consider something like political talk radio. All radio talk show hosts have the right to express their opinions, even if they do so in crass and fallacious ways. But we can still evaluate the reasoning and form of their communication as harmful or beneficial from the point of view of adding to or detracting from the aim to achieve the right answers and contribute to a flourishing community. Hence, the right to freedom of expression is not at risk when we negatively evaluate a class of expressions such as memes.

Many of the memes that one finds engaging in either fallacious reasoning or ostracizing the other are memes that also attempt to be humorous. Defenders may say that one cannot take these too seriously because they are meant to make people laugh and humor is a good thing. This raises the question of whether or not humor as a good can't be tainted by vicious effects. To put this another way, can the use of humor actually make an evil even more insidious in its effect? In addition, notice in the memes we have presented as ethically problematic, the humor may have a limited audience.

The claim, "It's only a joke," sometimes can be used as a deflecting reason in the attempt to ignore criticisms of some behavior or utterance. A person who criticizes a meme for its poor reasoning or wrongful treatment of a class of others may be told to, "lighten up, it's just a joke." And in many ways this is a conversation stopper meant to halt the criticism by making the critic feel like he or she is over-reacting. The fact that something is a joke doesn't always mean that it is unable to be criticized for its form, assumptions, and the message that it sends. Some jokes can be funny and morally questionable at the same time.

It is also the case that some morally questionable messages and the form of the reasoning expressed in or behind the jokes are more readily accepted and virally spread precisely because these things are couched in humor. Humor can help to spread ostracism. Think of racist and sexist jokes. They may be humorous to many while making the ostracism and poor treatment of the target class of people more acceptable within a culture. The same can happen with memes in that they could be humorous while making the mistreatment of the other or fallacious reasoning more tolerable within the wider community of social media users (which is a significant number of people and growing).

A final retort to the issues raised here is that we know the pernicious effects of rhetorical maneuvers on people's reasoning and its effect on the beliefs widely held in the community. As such, there is very little new in the case of memes in social media that we don't already confront in other forms of the mimetic expression, such as on bumper stickers and t-shirts. But we don't find bumper stickers and t-shirts pernicious. This seems like an attempt to have innocence by association, but it assumes that bumper stickers and t-shirts are unproblematic from the perspective of preserving the standards we want to meet in the community of sanity. Bumper stickers and t-shirts could be just as problematic as memes, but here are some reasons why we might think memes are more troublesome.

Memes are generated and passed with little investment on the part of users of social media; thus, generation and spread of memes is much more quickly to spread in ways that other forms of meme-like expression don't because they require persons to weigh the cost of purchasing or creating the expression versus its value to them as an expression of their personal views. Memes are cheap and quick to make and distribute. There is almost no personal cost in creating or sharing memes. Thus, less thought goes into the spread than may go into whether or not to buy a sticker or shirt, and to wear it. In addition, the feel of much social media is that it is informal and personal. Users are often much more likely to say or share things that they wouldn't put on their car or a t-shirt because of the sense of informality in much social media. This makes for a ripe atmosphere for many memes that are troublesome with regard to the aim of building and sustaining a community of sanity.

CONCLUSION

A guiding vision of a flourishing community includes a community that is dedicated to reasoning about difficult issues of deep human concern. The ideal community is able to reason and debate in a civil manner with each other because getting things right on hard issues is important to the well-being of the whole. Social media has completely penetrated the world we live in and it can be a media tool which either hinders or promotes the standards of thought and behavior conducive of flourishing communities. One possibly troublesome use of social media is the use of memes that model poor reasoning and discriminatory ideals, and which can impact users as they virally spread. These issues have been raised and analyzed. The concern that many may have is what to do about pernicious memes. First, it seems that users must be more reflective of what they post or share on their social media platforms. Second, that they be aware that although a meme may appear humorous it may not just be offensive, it can model forms of reasoning and attitudes of exclusion that are not conducive to a well-functioning society in a pluralistic world. Third, that they have courage to question friends (in a respectful way) who post memes which model intellectual and ethical behavior which are not reflective of having a community of sanity.

NOTES

1. I want to thank the organizers and participants in the September 2013 Jacksonville Philosophy Slam for the opportunity to test some of the ideas here and for their valuable feedback.
2. I want to thank Sarah Mattice for pointing out this element of some memes.

REFERENCES

McNeal, G. *Forbes Magazine OnLine*. Retrieved July 1, 2014 www.forbes.com/sites/gregorymcneal/2014/06/28/facebook-manipulated-user-news-feeds-to-create-emotional-contagion/.
Kant, I. (1956). *The Moral Law: Kant's Groundwork of the Metaphysic of Morals* (trans. H. J. Paton). London: Hutchinson University Library.
Levinas, E. (1969). *Totality and Infinity: An Essay on Exteriority* (trans. Alphonso Lingis). Pittsburgh: Duquesne University Press.
Putnam, H. (1990). *Realism with a Human Face*. Ed. James F. Conant. Cambridge, MA: Harvard University Press.
Sartre, J. P. (1943). *Being and Nothingness* (trans. H. E. Barnes) Editions Gallimard.

SEVEN

Living Well With a Foot in Each World

Deni Elliot and Frederick R. Carlson

Florida resident Meagan Simmons was arrested on a drunk driving charge July 25, 2010. She was booked at the Hillsborough County Jail and a mug shot was taken. As is usually the case with most public records, the mug shot was posted on the county website. Mug shots are rarely impressive, but this photo was an exception. The picture was a stunningly good headshot of Simmons. Mug shots are published by governmental entities as well as commercial operations. Some are re-publications by entrepreneurs that draw audiences to notable shots. Many of these re-publication sites also advertise a willingness to remove individual shots from their gallery for a price (Schwartz 2009). Simmons's mug shot went viral. By 2012, it was the subject of many meme-generated photos, which included these headlines: "Guilty of Taking My Breath Away," "Give Me Her Cell Number," and "Miss Demeanor." The Simmons picture generated hundreds, if not thousands of memes. The image, in various formats, traveled the Web, with Simmons picking up admirers as far as Norway and Australia (Moye 2013).

Initially, when Simmons learned of her Web popularity in 2013, she seemed amused. "If [Hugh Hefner] himself contacted me, I think that is an offer I cannot refuse," she told the *Huffington Post*, indicating that she'd model for *Playboy Magazine*. Simmons's mug shot brought more than 3,000 Twitter and Instagram followers to her accounts (Moye 2013).

Then the use of her picture became offensive to her. In 2014, Instant-CheckMate.com, a background checking service, used Simmons's mug shot to promote their website, running the mug shot photo with the caption, "Sometimes, the cute ones aren't so innocent. Do a background check on anyone" (Silman 2014).

Simmons sued InstantCheckMate.com for invasion of privacy. Simmons's attorney, Matthew Crist, said, "If someone is going to use your image, they need to pay you for it." In addition, in the text of the lawsuit, Simmons claimed that the exposure disturbed her peace of mind, invaded her privacy, and caused her anguish. So the photo that a year earlier elicited a chuckle from Simmons and launched a stronger social media presence for her was now being claimed as the cause of her "mental anguish" (Silman 2014). At the time of this writing, the lawsuit is pending.

It doesn't take a brush with the law to recognize that one's picture or identity has become an object easily found and freely taken by others for Internet-based use. Many people have faced some consequence of having photos taken of them without their knowledge and posted on public websites without their consent. More than one person has been dismayed to find that those photos were accessible to current and potential employers as well as shocked loved ones. Fun at a private party can easily end up as Internet fodder.

Welcome to the brave new world of living life in public. The ease of posting information about one's friends, enemies, and strangers coupled with the lack of awareness of the consequences of posting information about oneself has led to physical, psychological, financial, and reputational harm for some people. The posting of identifiable information about persons caught up in newsworthy events, including children, has created an eternal Internet hell for others.

This chapter seeks to answer two questions: "How has advancing technology changed reasonable expectations of privacy? Is it possible to really live what philosophers describe as *the good life* if individuals cannot control the access of others to their virtual world movements or control the use of information by others?" The liberty and property aspects of privacy rights have been argued to express both philosophically based freedoms and psychologically required aspects of human existence (Moore 2010).

These are important questions because technology at the turn of the twenty-first century has profoundly changed the way that people interact with information and with one another. Anyone who has records kept by a governmental agency, including educational systems, IRS, and Social Security, or who has a credit or debit card is living life in an electronically based public domain, whether they like it or not. Electronic and networked recordkeeping means that people are tracked and open to review in ways that were impossible before the turn of the twenty-first century. According to one scholar, "Nearly three-quarters of American job recruiters report that they have rejected candidates because of information found online, such as photos and social-networking sites—material many of us might assume is private" (Plaisance 2013). Whatever the notion of privacy may mean in contemporary society, it cannot include a notion of invisibility. Is the good life achievable if one cannot escape having a public persona?

PHILOSOPHICAL NOTIONS OF THE GOOD LIFE

If we assume, as Aristotle did, that the good life consists of human flourishing the question that flows from these precepts is how, or if, technology reinforces the good life. The purpose of this section is to understand the good life through three snapshots over time: Aristotle's description of more than two thousand years ago, as he was the first philosopher to fully address the notion in writing, the enlightenment philosophy of John Stuart Mill, upon whom many of our Western notions of good government and citizenship are based, and a contemporary philosopher of technology, Albert Borgmann, who addresses the ethical issues of human use of technology directly.[1]

Aristotle

We begin with Aristotle. The concept of the good life was coined by Aristotle and described throughout his works, but most particularly in *Politics* and *Nicomachean Ethics*. There were several tenets of this philosophical construct.

First, people are, by nature, political and social animals. We can't become our own best selves without citizenship, interaction, and community. One cannot fully develop as a human being and thus have a good life without connection to community.

Second, rational contemplation is the key to becoming the best person possible; but rationalism must be balanced with other aspects of human experience, such as the fulfillment of appetite and desire. It is fine to satisfy our appetites for sustenance and sex; it is okay to go after the many objects of human desire. But we must control these "animalistic" motivators by exercising moderation. The only thing a person can't have too much of, according to Aristotle, is wisdom, the outcome of rational thought and contemplation. Meeting appetites and desires in moderation and seeking wisdom is how harmony in the soul, or what we'd call today "balance" or "being centered," is achieved.

Third, a person cannot achieve happiness by striving for it. When we are performing all of the functions that give us "the good life"—rationality, being active in community, and being moderate in how we satisfy our appetites and desires—we realize that we are happy. Happiness is not an end that can be pursued in itself.

Fourth, people develop character through practice and by acquiring the right habits. For example, one becomes truthful by practicing being truthful until telling the truth becomes a habit. A person becomes courageous by doing courageous acts until doing so does not take any internal struggle.

Fifth, the ideal community maximizes the happiness of citizens, in part by establishing laws that help people develop the habits necessary to become good citizens. Developing the right habits frees our thinking so that we're able to identify and attend to difficult ethical issues.

Last, friends are important but they need to be the right kind of friends. True friends encourage one another to be morally better than they would otherwise be. If the moral development between people is uneven, then true friendship is impossible. A person who you call a friend because that person is useful to you or merely brings you pleasure is not a true friend. You must befriend one another with the goal of helping the other become the best person that he or she can be.

Aristotle counsels that we need to seek practical wisdom, interact with others, and choose our friends carefully if we are going to live the good life.

John Stuart Mill

Moving through time to the nineteenth-century British philosopher John Stuart Mill, we see the importance of individuals and community interaction more sharply focused. Mill gives us more specific steps to determine how to achieve the good life. Like Aristotle, Mill believes that understanding the ultimate goal for one's fulfillment or self-actualization can provide a road map for how one ought to live. Like Aristotle, Mill believes that true happiness for individuals comes about when they live the most fully human experience. A good understanding of Mill's plan for the good life can be found through a careful reading of his two best known works: *On Liberty* and *Utilitarianism*. Mill's fully developed people are those who understand that their own happiness is based on the good of the community and that the only way that an individual can be truly happy is in active involvement in making the world a better place. This profoundly social conception of the good life has a number of important factors.

First, happiness is not simply the satisfaction of one's appetites or short-term pleasure. As in Aristotle's description, happiness adheres to the ability of people to think rationally. Mill says, "It is better to be a human being dissatisfied than a pig satisfied; better to be Socrates dissatisfied than a fool satisfied. And, if the fool, or the pig, is of a different opinion, it is because they only know their side of the question. The other party to the comparison knows both sides" (1863; 1991, 140).

Next, through education and experience, people see themselves as necessarily involved in making the community better. These morally developed individuals come to understand that they can't be happy living in a community in which others suffer. They must do something to help. Mill says,

> All the grand sources, in short, of human suffering are in a great degree, many of them almost entirely, conquerable by human care and effort; and though their removal is grievously slow . . . yet every man sufficiently intelligent and generous to bear a part, however small and unconspicuous in the endeavor, will draw a noble enjoyment from the contest itself, which he would not for any bribe in the form of selfish indulgence consent to be without. (1863; 1991, 146)

Third, individuals have a moral duty to "seek the truest opinion possible" (Mill 1859, in Gray 1991, 42–43). Mill contended that most people don't know what they really believe. We spout beliefs, but have not taken the time to examine what supports our beliefs and what argues against them. People naturally have a tendency of selective exposure. We think we know what we believe. We reinforce our beliefs by surrounding ourselves with other people and information that support our beliefs. Therefore, Mill concludes that most people "have never thrown themselves into the mental position of those who think differently from them, and consider what such persons may have to say; and consequently they do not, in any proper sense of the word, know the doctrine which they themselves profess" (1859; 1991, 42–43). The other essential in seeking the truest opinion possible is in accepting that one's deeply held beliefs may be wrong or incomplete. Living the good life, according to Mill, requires being involved in creating a better world, valuing the happiness of other people in community as one values one's own, and keeping an open mind so that it is possible to learn from facts and from the opinions of others.

Albert Borgmann

Unlike these earlier philosophers, Borgmann specifically addresses technology as a force that can pull against an individual's ability to achieve the good life. People don't have to choose between technology or the good life. On the other hand, it ought not be assumed that technology that makes our lives easier automatically leads to the good life. Like the other philosophers, Borgmann rests his arguments on individual ability to live life consciously and make choices that keep us on the path toward self-actualization. Technology, in some instances, can help. In other instances, technology hinders one's progress. If technology is not used consciously and with a full understanding of its costs and benefits, technology ceases to be a tool that people use and instead becomes a force that rules how people spend their time, attention, and energy.

Borgmann's list of what constitutes a good life is inherently relational, social, and active. As with Aristotle and Mill, the good life is dependent upon bringing rationality to the choices one makes. But rather than struggle against one's own desires and appetites, the struggle Borgmann describes is against the *device paradigm* (Borgmann 1984). Devices, which are people-created instruments, including hardware and software, are those that help people accomplish their goals. The problematic devices are those that can disappear behind their functions. The device paradigm is the structuring of life by government and corporations, with individuals' acquiescence that creates distance between the manufacture or development of goods and services and the consuming of those goods and services.

Amazon.com is an easy example. The act of shopping is easier online than going to the store. Shopping at Amazon.com does not require that we engage with merchants or adjust our desires to an inventory restricted by what the store shelf can hold. But in the process of buying goods the easy, online way, a number of devices necessary to the process become hidden or unobtrusive. For example, an online shopping site displays a purposeful hierarchy of items. What that hierarchy represents, in terms of profits, corporate partnerships, or even the corporation's assessment of what an individual consumer might buy, is easy to ignore as long as shoppers find what satisfies them in one or two mouse clicks. The human cost and other resource costs involved in making the items and in having them available universally is distant and irrelevant to one's purchase.

Even spending money online is unobtrusive and uses a networking device that is hidden as compared to the physical action of exchanging currency for goods. A mouse click confirms purchase, but monetary consequence for the purchase is delayed until the credit card's billing date. There is no experience of having spent money in real time or of facing the consequences of spending money in real time. Without conscious involvement and real-life/real-time engagement, the device paradigm creates a technological creep so that it is difficult for individuals to even notice when virtual ease has substituted for engagement with others.

Next, the good life is "oriented by focal things, concerns and practices in the context of a household, of family life" (Wood 2003). "A focal thing is something that has a commanding presence, engages your body and mind, and engages you with others. . . . A focal practice results from committed engagement with the focal thing" (Wood 2003). Borgmann uses a guitar as an example for a focal thing. It requires a certain kind of engagement of body and mind and as one learns to play it, the individual is united with "the larger tradition of music and the community of musicians." The good life, according to Borgmann, consists of active engagement rather than passive reception. Instead of passively taking in entertainment, for example, the good life consists of actively creating entertainment. Making music rather than simply listening to music; telling and listening to stories in real-life face-to-face conversation rather than passively ingesting them through television or online; getting out into the world, seeking, noticing, and learning new skills through interaction, rather than watching someone else do it on television or in a YouTube video.

Third, technology is insidious and can replace focal practice without an individual's notice. Borgmann explains, "In the case of television, information and entertainment become easily available. . . . If two or three hours of television a day come into our lives, then something else has to go out. And what has gone out? Telling stories, reading, going to the theater, socializing with friends, just taking a walk to see what's up in the neighborhood" (Wood 2003). So, while technology has freed us of some burdens that are beneficial to people and community, such as health problems, it is not okay for technology to take away all of the burdens that accompany active involvement in real life. The "burden" of communally preparing a meal, eating together, and cleaning up, for example, comes with benefits for human relationships. Such activity connects us historically to culture and family. It connects us directly to the foods we eat, their origins, and how they are prepared. The further we move away from direct involvement in procuring, preparing, and ingesting an actual fruit, vegetable, or animal product in its natural form, the less connected we are to our bodies, family, and life in general. Eating processed or fast food in front of the television dissuades us from activities that promote the good life. The good life is not a relative concept. It is not up to each person to decide for him or herself what constitutes the good. Seeking the good life requires "a meaningful examination of our culture, which inevitably is a common and collective enterprise" (Wood 2003). As with Mill, the struggle to become a fully flourishing human being includes interaction with others.

Last, experience of the physical world is necessary to live the good life. Virtual activity, according to Borgmann, is *derivative*. On the Internet, an individual is not directly in touch with another human being. Your virtual interaction is dependent on individual's beliefs about an online persona's physical identity. I may think that the customer service representative, with whom I am having an "online live chat" as having a particular gender, age, location, but all of this is pure projection on my part. It is possible that I am wrong with all of these guesses. Indeed, the "person" who I think is helping me with my problem may be a chatterbot—a robot created to provide assistance and mimic human interaction.

Virtual ambiguity is dense and thick. It is true, as the old saying goes, "On the Internet, no one knows you are a dog." Yet meaningful human interaction is reinforced in a constant loop of feedback and projection. Living the good life is not possible, according to Borgmann, without the reality testing of interaction with people in the physical world. His answer is not to turn our backs on technology, but rather to control our use of technology so that technology doesn't control our lives. Individuals must actively and consciously protect their lives and those of their children's in the physical world so that natural and cultural ecologies can develop and flourish. In short, more Little League, less Screen Time.

To summarize these philosophers, the Internet is not, metaphorically, a town square. Retrieved data is not knowledge. Facebook friends are not friends. Calling technology a tool denies its power. As media scholar Clifford Christians explained, "The philosophical rationale for human action is reverence for life on earth, for the organic whole, for the physical realm in which human civilization is situated . . . technological products are legitimate if and only if they maintain cultural continuity (Christians, quoted in Plaisance 2014).

PRIVACY: FROM PHOTOGRAPHY TO THE "NETWORKING OF EVERYTHING"

As the virtual world grows, so does the general public's, government's, and business' access to one's personal information. Proponents of public and transparent life sometimes refer to the good old days when people lived their lives in small towns and everyone knew everybody's business. The argument is that virtual disclosure is not so different from all the town's people shopping at the local general store and seeing who is strolling down the boulevard with whom. Thus, stumbling across a person you know at the local coffee shop is equated with the virtual collection and distribution of data. Philosopher John Barlow said of small town life, "What makes the fishbowl community tolerable is a general willingness of small towns to forgive in their own way all that should be forgiven. The individual is protected from the malice of his fellows, not by their lack of dangerous information about him, but by their disinclination to use it" (Barlow 1991).

While Barlow attempts to show how the Internet is like a small town, there are problems with this analogy. Communities in the physical world exist for human flourishing. Spaces in the virtual world exist for corporate flourishing. In the physical world, individuals exercise at least a limited liberty right to move about without being intentionally followed and a limited property right to choose with whom to share information about themselves. In contrast, when individuals participate in the virtual world, they automatically pay to do so by revealing details of their physical world identities as well as by automatically leaving tracks that reveals each online movement. Living in a small town in the physical world guarantees real-time connection and interaction with the others who live there. Neighbors know complete people, not photos, quips, and data that make up online persona.

Legal limits and ethical conventions developed over the twentieth century to create a boundary between casual observation and stalking. Law and ethics recognizes the difference between gossip and intentional disclosure of private facts about an individual (LII / Legal Information Institute 2014). People share secrets with those closest to them. How those secrets are shared is no longer in the originator's control. But if someone were to broadcast a private individual's secret known to fewer than fifty other people to the world at large, the broadcaster may be legally liable for disclosure of private facts. And, as Barlow suggests, knowing individuals fully in real life suggests an equivalent level of disclosure on all sides. We learn to forgive and let go of quirks, unfortunate events, even those times in which an individual may be drunk or enraged or otherwise out of control. Online, those moments may be all that we see of a person; his or her online persona substitutes for our experience of the real person.

The ability to share visual information has raised both privacy concerns and infliction of emotional harm from the beginning. In 1890, Supreme Court Justices Samuel D. Warren and Louis D. Brandeis provided the first formal comprehensive analysis of the right to be left alone. In their *Harvard Law Review* article, they wrote,

> Recent inventions and business methods call attention to the next step which must be taken for the protection of the person, and for securing to the individual what Judge Cooley calls "the right to be left alone." Instantaneous photographs and newspaper enterprise have invaded the sacred precedents of private and domestic life; and numerous mechanical devices threaten to make good the prediction that "what is whispered in the closet shall be proclaimed from the house-tops." (Warren and Brandeis 1890)

The ways that privacy can be invaded have multiplied as technology as evolved. Undoubtedly, many people have been caused emotional harm when content intended for a small chosen audience is spread beyond that group. A case that shows how fine the nuances can be when it comes to legal decisions in such a matter in such a claim is illustrative.

In 1993, Dan Boyles, then seventeen, with the help of two friends set up a video camera to record him and his nineteen-year-old girlfriend, Susan Leigh Kerr, having sex. Boyles shared the recording with ten of his friends. Kerr did not approve of Boyles sharing the tape with those ten friends and it is possible that the tape was shared beyond that group. When Kerr discovered that the recording had been shared, six months after the fact, she demanded the return of the tape (Scott 1995). Boyles returned the tape as requested. Ultimately, Kerr decided not to sue for disclosure of private facts, but successfully sued Boyles for negligent in-

fliction of emotional distress at the trial and initial appeals level. Ultimately, she lost at the Texas Supreme Court level (Cerasuolo 1993). The
Supreme Court found that Kerr's claim that Boyles had "negligently"
inflicted emotional distress was too broad. The Court's problem was with
the categorization of the harm as based on negligence. People are harmed
by insensitivity or rude behavior, but those are not actionable claims. The
Court remanded the decision back to District Court, suggesting that Kerr
could have a finding of fact and law based on "intentional" rather than
"negligent" inflection of emotional harm. So, although the Supreme
Court suggested that Boyles' action rose to this higher standard of infliction of harm, Kerr declined to re-file the suit (Cerasuolo 1993).

Sometimes public interest can override privacy claims, even if the
technology is used to spy in one's own backyard. Take the 1990 case of
Blevins v. Sorrell. Homer Sorrell and Chalmers Brewer suspected that
their noisy next-door neighbors, Richard and Jennifer Blevins, were running a lawn mower repair business, which violated zoning regulations.
In order to get evidence, Sorrell and Brewer set up a telescope with a
connected camera to monitor activity in Blevins's backyard. The Blevins
responded by constructing a privacy fence. Sorrell and Brewster built a
tall platform for their equipment. They recorded over the privacy fence.
The court found that Sorrell and Brewer had a qualified privilege to
check to see if Blevins was violating town ordinances (Scott 1995). The
court reasoned that Sorrell and Brewer did not act out of bad faith or
reckless disregard in their surveillance of Blevins (Blevins 1990).

Telephoto photography has evolved into pictures snapped from space
and on the street with no human intention or control. Cases filed against
Google maps for claimed invasions of privacy have generally not been
successful. Just as Sorrell and Brewster were found to have a qualified
privilege to peer over their neighbor's privacy fence for the public interest, Google, too, has been allowed to continue to snap pictures and publish them online despite the fact that the cameras, situated seven to eight
feet off the ground, can "see" over hedges that would block street-level
view. Google now blurs faces and license plates, and will remove content
that others report as objectionable, but maintains that what its cameras
can snap in the physical world is for a global virtual audience to see.

TECHNOLOGY AND PRIVACY IN TODAY'S WORLD

Technology situates people as simultaneously citizens of both the physical and virtual worlds. There is no longer any boundary between the
worlds that would make privacy claims legitimate in one world and not
in the other. This section provides examples of how technological capabilities merge virtual data and real-life experience into a seamless and
multi-faceted publicly accessed portrait of people who would have once

been thought to be private individuals. Some of these technologies are those directly used by consumers, such as cellular photo sharing. Others, such as the manipulation and storage of data, are less visible to consumers, but have great impact on what others know about them.

Shared Mobile Photography

Mobile photography, such as pictures taken via a cellphone, can create privacy issues if users do not know their default sharing settings or if someone with whom a photo is shared turns out to be less than trustworthy. Hunter Moore was the self-proclaimed "King of Revenge Porn," until he shut down his site *Is Anyone Up?* in response to threats of lawsuits. The site was mostly "user-generated content." Sometimes Moore found pictures that were unintentionally published on public sites. More often, ex-boyfriends or ex-husbands posted pictures on Moore's site that were pictures that had been snapped by the subject herself or taken by her partner with consent. The intent of publishing on *Is Anyone Up?* or other revenge porn sites was to cause psychological or reputational harm to the photo's subject. Moore said he launched the site for "public humiliation," and called himself a "professional life-ruiner" (Holpuch 2014). Every digitized photo we take with our cellular phones has the potential to be placed on the Internet, where they live forever and can be resurrected at any time. The site was eventually brought down by a $250,000 judgment that paved the way for aggressive action by the FBI. Moore threatened to rape the wife of James McGibney, an "antibullying" website owner, and called him a pedophile on numerous occasions (Alfonso 2013). The FBI then arrested Moore on charges of conspiracy and aggravated identity theft.

Mobile Remote Sensors

Mobile remote sensors come in many forms. Robotic drone aircraft, wearable sensors, or vehicle-mounted sensors are common platforms. Robotic drone aircraft are remotely piloted airframes and are best known for their role in the military. Wearable sensors are networked connected devices that can send data throughout the Internet. The most well-known example of wearable sensors is the Google Glass product, which is a networked video camera attached to eyeglasses. Vehicle-mounted sensors are video, audio, and telemetry devices that are attached to vehicles. The Google Street View project makes extensive use of vehicle-mounted sensors. Media scholar Kathleen Culver described four ways that news organizations are likely to use drone technology to capture newsworthy events: aerial images, live-streamed video, digital mapping, and analytic data. These abilities impact conventional beliefs about privacy. She said, "In the same way telephoto lenses extended the perimeter from which photos could be taken, drones can alter the space from which images and data can feasibly be captured. For instance, a person has no reasonable expectation of privacy on a public beach, but many would object to the practice of a news organization using a drone to capture an ongoing all-day livestream of a beach for constant broadcast (Culver 2013). Drone technology for newsgathering, like Google Maps, adds the possibility that one's recorded image might be broadcast widely or be accessible on the Internet. Societies' idea of what counts as public has expanded as more public areas can be captured and displayed.

Data Mining of Search and User Behavior

Data mining, and the monetization of user data, is key to the business of social media companies. Large-scale data analysis creates significant privacy concerns because users can now inexpensively get to data in ways that even a large organization could not do just a few years ago. The ability to combine data from different sources and conduct sophisticated data analysis using cheap (or free) tools creates a significant change in our expectation of privacy.

Joshua Fairfield and Hannah Shtein have introduced the concept of "informational harm" (Fairfield and Shtein 2013), to suggest that collapsing data to develop information about a person might result in a problematic portrait that would not otherwise be possible. Data mining ties other sensor data and content to create a unified visualization of behavior. The goal of the social media business and other organizations is to know your behavior in great detail for their own commercial goals. The Federal Trade Commission recently released a report that found that the nine major data brokerage firms were targeting their customer's online data by race, income, and "health interest," which is a legal code word for searching for medical conditions such as diabetes (Faturechi 2014). This harvesting of data may be in direct conflict with individual privacy concerns.

Viral Nature of Photographic and Video Distribution

The technology that stores and forwards content in social media is, in itself, a concern. From the early days of the Internet, the business proposition behind Internet advertising is a "viral" model. The rapid movement of social media content is caused by millions of people and machines forwarding content independent of one another. The result is an extraordinarily rapid propagation of crowd- and corporate-sourced content. A study in 2012 by Facebook/University of Michigan looked at the signals among 253 million people on Facebook. The researchers found that the diffusion of information was mostly based on many users pushing content through the system. To push the content means to send content from a source to the end user, who is a recipient of the content. The research also made a distinction between users with "Strong Ties" and "Weak Ties." The distinction is based on the number of links each user has and the amount of content pushed through those links. Users with Strong Ties may have provided the initial push for content to be viewed, but it was the users with Weak Ties who provided the persistence, or the amount of time and reach ("diffusion") the noticeable content remains engaged (Bakshy 2012).

Internet of Things (IoT)

The Internet of Things is a term used to describe the tagging of objects, animals, and people with an address and a connection mechanism to the Internet. The term "überveillance" describes an extreme extension of the Internet of Things. According to Michael and Michael,

> Überveillance is more than closed circuit television feeds, or cross-agency databases linked to national identity cards, or biometrics and ePassports used for international travel. Überveillance is the sum total of all these types of surveillance and the deliberate integration of an individual's personal data for the continuous tracking and monitoring of identity and location in real time. (Michael and Michael 2007)

An example of this continuous tracking is the "M7 Processor" that is in the Apple iPhone 5S. This processor, along with a program called Core-Motion, allows the phone to continually collect data from the accelerometer, gyroscope, and compass. The M7 is always on, even when the phone is seemingly powered off (Estes 2013).

Current applications of IoT include the creation of media platforms to interconnect security systems and home appliances to social media, monitor the elderly, and use radio frequency identification (RFID) tagging for animal tracking and identification. Überveillance takes the next step. Michael and Michael posit a future where the human being becomes a continuously tracked entity. Increasingly, devices communicate and share information within the larger Internet network. Those connections can add to the unified vision of search and behavior tracking that is the goal of many data mining and social media organizations. The concern is not just governmental surveillance, but commercial surveillance intent on exploiting individuals' consumptive behavior. If trends continue, this involves a total relinquishment of the liberty aspect of privacy.

CONCLUSION

We now return to Meagan Simmons. Her case is particularly noteworthy because it exemplifies the permanence and speed that accompany online disclosure of information. The sensor used to create her digital photo was a deputy at the Hillsborough County Jail acting in legitimate ways. But the results from legitimate disclosure of information cannot be controlled. No one associated with sharing Meagan Simmons's mug shot did anything legally wrong, aside from, possibly, the entity using her photo for the company's financial gain. It is likely that no individual slapping a humorous headline on the mug shot of a stranger and sending it along a network had any thought that there might be an ethical issue with doing so.

In our contemporary web of virtual and physical reality, we must redefine our ethical conventions of how we treat one another, even people we do not know. The good news is that continued experience in the physical world can remind us of actions in the virtual world that promote human flourishing for ourselves and others. People are vulnerable. They can be harmed. With the individual's ability to publish data found or created throughout the world, people have unprecedented power to cause harm. Just as we respect ethical conventions and do not go out of our way to cause harm to individuals in the physical world, we should not cause harm to individuals in the virtual world. People need to understand that behind the meme-generated photo, there is a real person who may not have had any control of a picture going viral.

Instead of depending on emerging law to protect one's privacy, as law comes with the double effect of limiting the publication of legitimate material, individuals need to be conscious of their own self-disclosure and the ethics of sharing information from and about others. Data shared is privacy lost. A request for information does not obligate an answer. Resist telling tales online, even about one's worst enemy. Humankind learned to adjust to the intrusive nature of still photography in the hands of government, corporations, and individuals. Transparency of one's self and actions is not necessarily the death of privacy. The unwillingness to consider the consequences of sharing data about individuals may be. So the answer to whether one can live the good life in public is a qualified "Yes." Living with increased exposure requires the collaboration among individuals and the control of government and corporations so that exposure doesn't lead to exploitation.

Engaging in real-world relationships, as Borgmann mandates, serves as a good reminder that real people can be harmed through Internet-based information, even if the virtual-world experience of them feels far from real flesh and real time. Virtual world "friends" are not friends in any philosophically relevant sense unless knowledge of them is accompanied by physical world contact in real time. Even then, recognizing a true friend is dependent on what each does to promote the moral growth and development of the other. Shopping in real time at local stores reminds us that consumers are not required to disclose their contact information to make a cash purchase, even if that information is requested.

Living well in today's society requires individuals keep one foot in the physical world and one in the virtual. Refusing to be a citizen of the global world is denial of contemporary reality and abdication of one's moral responsibilities. Conscious use of the virtual world provides unprecedented opportunities for individuals to become the engaged, active citizens that philosophers say is also necessary for the good life.

Media organizations need to exert self-regulation over what they publish on the Internet. Codes of ethics, first written by media organizations in the 1920s, are based on the appreciation that one's legal freedom does not imply an act is ethical. Children should not be identified in a news story in any way that might affect them personally or professionally in adulthood. News organizations should reconsider if the revenue brought in by publishing mug shots to draw audience to their sites is worth the loss of good will or of being an unintended accomplice in the spread of meme-generated photos.

Citizens, through legislative action, should hold corporations accountable for the collection and use of data regarding individuals. Unknowingly, or with little thought, individuals sign site agreements that allow corporate use of their data for commercial purposes. The virtual world was created to serve commercial interests and its important citizens recognize the dangers of living in a virtual Times Square. As an example, it ought not be required for individuals to reveal their real names or physical world identities to engage in online activities. Rather, corporations have a responsibility to justify the collection of that data. Increasing their profits or manipulating individual's data for commercial purposes is not a good enough reason.

Aristotle argued that the good life was possible only if a person is engaged and active in civic life. Mill argued that the attainment of one's own moral development is possible only through public discussion in which our ideas and beliefs are constantly challenged. Via the internet we have unparalleled opportunities to seek views that are different from our own and test our own opinions and ideas. A plethora of evidence, opinion, and discussion opportunities are available for anyone with Internet access.

The web shines light on every corner of the world. We cannot hide behind ignorance of the human condition. From working with charities that address the world's great calamities to contributing to intensely local websites that tell neighbors where to find free fallen fruit, individuals can make a difference in the world as Mill counsels they should. The virtual world can serve as a vehicle for individual flourishing and attainment of the good life. Individuals can maintain personal identity regardless of the public stare. But to do so, individuals must control technology rather than allowing technology to control them.

NOTES

1. Historically, philosophical writings reflect the sexism and classism of the time and place in which they were written. Aside from direct quotes, the interpretation in this chapter is written to be inclusive of humankind.

REFERENCES

18 U.S. Code § 2261A—Stalking. LII / Legal Information Institute. Retrieved April 10, 2014 from www.law.cornell.edu/uscode/text/18/2261A.

About Precision Drone. Retrieved April 12, 2014 from www.precisiondrone.com/.

Alfonso III, F. (2013, March 11). "Revenge Porn King Hunter Moore Fined $250,000 in Defamation Suit." *The Daily Dot*. Retrieved June 5, 2014 from www.dailydot.com/news/hunter-moore-revenge-porn-defamation-lawsuit.

Bakshy, E., Rosenn, I., Marlow, C., and L. Adamic. (2012, February 28). "The Role of Social Networks in Information Diffusion." Retrieved April 12, 2014 from arxiv.org/abs/1201.4145.

Barcella, L. (2003, June 30). "Harsh Reality: Unwitting Traveler Takes 'Candid Camera' to Court." Retrieved April 12, 2014, from news.findlaw.com/court_tv/s/20030620/20jun2003193840.html.

Barlow, J. P. (1991, June). "Private Life in Cyberspace." *Communications of the ACM*. Retrieved from w2.eff.org/Misc/Publications/John_Perry_Barlow/HTML/complete_acm_columns.html#private.

Behind the Scenes—Street View. (2014). About Street View. Retrieved June 5, 2014, from www.google.com/maps/about/behind-the-scenes/streetview/.

Bell, E. (2012, September 5). "Journalism by Numbers." *Columbia Journalism Review*. Retrieved April 12, 2014, from www.cjr.org/cover_story/journalism_by_numbers.php?page=all.

Blevins v. Sorrell (Court of Appeals of Ohio, Warren County July 23, 1990) (Leagle, Dist. file).

Borgmann, A. (1984). *Technology and the Character of Contemporary Life: A Philosophical Inquiry*. Chicago: University of Chicago Press.

Borgmann, A. (1999). *Holding on to Reality: The Nature of Information at the Turn of the Millennium*. Chicago: University of Chicago Press.

Borgmann, A. (2013). "So Who Am I Really? Personal Identity in the Age of the Internet." *Ai & Society* 28, no. 1 (February): 15–20. doi:10.1007/s00146-012-0388-0.

Cadwalladr, C. (2014, March 30). "Charlotte Laws' Fight with Hunter Moore, the Internet's Revenge Porn King." *The Observer*. Retrieved April 11, 2014, from www.theguardian.com/culture/2014/mar/30/charlotte-laws-fight-with-internet-revenge-porn-king.

Campion, S., and H. Hojek. (2014, April 3). "Hidden Camera Found in Vacation Home on Fort Myers Beach." NBC-2.com WBBH News for Fort Myers, Cape Coral & Naples, Florida. Retrieved April 12, 2014, from www.nbc-2.com/story/25132930/hidden-camera-found-in-vacation-home-on-fort-myers-beach#.U8W3QJRdXTo.

Cerasuolo, G. F. (1993). "Boyles v. Kerr Sex, Emotional Distress, and Videotape." *Houston Law Review*. Retrieved April 15, 2014, from LexusNexus.

Cha, M., Mislove, A., and K. Gummadi. (2009). "A Measurement-Driven Analysis of Information Propagation in the Flickr Social Network." Proceedings of WWW 2009, Madrid, Spain. Retrieved April 6, 2014, from www.mpi-sws.org/~gummadi/papers/www09-cha.pdf.

Churchill, S. (2010, November 9). "UAVs: Flying Cell Towers." *Dailywireless.org*. Retrieved April 12, 2014, from www.dailywireless.org/2012/11/19/uavs-flying-cell-towers/.

Culver, K. B. (2014). "From Battlefield to Newsroom: Ethical Implications of Drone Technology in Journalism." *Journal of Mass Media Ethics* 29, no. 1 (January 2, 2014): 52–64. doi:10.1080/08900523.2013.829679.

Dodero, Camille. (2012, April 4). "Hunter Moore Makes a Living Screwing You." Villagevoice.com. Retrieved April 12, 2014, from www.villagevoice.com/2012-04-04/news/revenge-porn-hunter-moore-is-anyone-up/2/.

Estes, A. (2013, September 10). "How Apple's M7 Chip Makes the IPhone 5S the Ultimate Tracking Device." *Gizmodo.* Retrieved June 5, 2014 from gizmodo.com/how-apples-m7-chip-makes-the-iphone-5s-the-ultimate-tr-1286594287.

Fairfield, J., and H. Shtein. (2014). "Big Data, Big Problems: Emerging Issues in the Ethics of Data Science and Journalism." *Journal of Mass Media Ethics* 29, no. 1 (January 2): 38–51. doi:10.1080/08900523.2014.863126.

Faturechi, R. (2014, May 27). "Data Brokers Are Profiling Consumers Online by Race, Other Categories." *Los Angeles Times.* Retrieved June 5, 2014 from www.latimes.com/business/technology/la-fi-tn-data-brokers-ftc-20140527-story.html.

Holpuch, A. (2014, January 23). "FBI Arrest and Charge Revenge Porn Mogul Hunter Moore." Theguardian.com. Retrieved April 12, 2014, from www.theguardian.com/culture/2014/jan/23/fbi-arrest-and-charge-revenge-porn-mogul-hunter-moore.

Michael, M. G., and K. Michael. (2007). "A Note on Überveillance / A Note on Uberveillance." *Proceedings of the Second Workshop on Social Implications of National Security, Wollongong, Australia.* Retrieved April 6, 2014 from ro.uow.edu.au/cgi/viewcontent.cgi?article=1558&context=infopapers.

Mill, J. S. (2008) "Utilitarianism." In *On Liberty and Other Essays*, John Gray (Ed.). Oxford: Oxford University Press.

Moore, A. D. (2010). "Defining Privacy." In *Privacy Rights: Moral and Legal Foundations*, 11–32. University Park, PA: Pennsylvania State University Press.

Moye, D. (2013, April 9). "Meagan Simmons, 'Attractive Convict,' Comes To Grips With Mug Shot Meme, Says She'd Do Playboy." TheHuffingtonPost.com. Retrieved April 12, 2014, from www.huffingtonpost.com/2013/04/09/meagan-simmons-attractive_n_3045604.html.

MU IT Program Drone Lab. Retrieved April 12, 2014, from dronelab.missouri.edu/drone-journalism/.

Murray, R. (2010, April 20). "IsAnyoneUp? Shuts Down: 'Revenge Porn' Forum Bought by Anti-bullying Website." nydailynews.com. Retrieved April 12, 2014 from www.nydailynews.com/news/money/isanyoneup-shuts-revenge-porn-forum-bought-anti-bullying-website-article-1.1064608.

"Nir Rosen Apologizes, Resigns From NYU Over 'Cruel And Insensitive' Lara Logan Tweets." (2011, February 16). Newyorkcbslocal.com. Retrieved April 12, 2014, from newyork.cbslocal.com/2011/02/16/nir-rosen-apologizes-resigns-from-nyu-over-lara-logan-tweets/.

Palen, L., Salzman, M., and E. Youngs. (2000). "Going Wireless: Behavior & Practice of New Mobile Phone Users." Retrieved April 6, 2014, www.cs.colorado.edu/~palen/Papers/cscwPalen.pdf.

Pelisek, C. (2011, October 13). "Celebrities' Email Hacking Nightmare." Thedailybeast.com. retrieved April 12, 2014, from www.thedailybeast.com/articles/2011/10/13/scarlett-johannson-photo-arrest-latest-in-fbi-war-against-hackers.html.

Plaisance, P. L. (2009). "Technology." In *Media Ethics: Key Principles for Responsible Practice*, 55–70. Los Angeles: SAGE.

Plaisance, P. L. (2013). "Virtue Ethics and Digital 'Flourishing': An Application of Philippa Foot to Life Online." *Journal of Mass Media Ethics* 28, no. 2 (2013): 91–102. doi:10.1080/08900523.2013.792691.

Schnurmacher, E. C. (1935, September 1). "Wire That Picture." *Popular Mechanics.* Retrieved April 12, 2014, from books.google.com.

Schwartz, B. (2009, October 15). "Get Out Of Google Jail For $50, Web Site Captures Mug Shots." Seroundtable.com. Retrieved April 12, 2014, from www.seroundtable.com/archives/020959.html.

Scott, G. G. (1995). "Keeping Watch." In *Mind Your Own Business: The Battle for Personal Privacy*, 325–41. New York: Insight Books.

Silman, J. (2014, February 27). "Woman behind 'attractive Convict' Mug Shot Sues for Invasion of Privacy." tampabay.com. Retrieved April 12, 2014. www.tampabay.com/news/courts/civil/zephyrhills-woman-in-attractive-convict-mugshot-files-suit/2167688.

Spy Tec Equipment Shop. Hidden Cameras. Retrieved April 12, 2014, from www.spytecinc.com/video-devices/nanny-cams-hidden-came-ra.html?gclid=CLP11sPWx70CFSwdOgodpxgABg.

"Streisand Sues Photographer for Posting Pictures of Malibu Estate." (2003, June 5). *Reporters Committee for Freedom of the Press*. Retrieved April 12, 2014, from www.rcfp.org/browse-media-law-resources/news/streisand-sues-photographer-posting-pictures-malibu-estate.

Streitfeld, D. (2013, March 12). "Google Concedes That Drive-By Prying Violated Privacy." nytimes.com. Retrieved April 12, 2014, from www.nytimes.com/2013/03/13/technology/google-pays-fine-over-street-view-privacy-breach.html?_r=0.

United States Government. Department of Transportation. Federal Aviation Administration. *Unmanned Aircraft System Test Site*. CFR ed. Vol. 14. Part 91.

Warren, S. D., and L. D. Brandeis. (1890). "The Right to Privacy." *Harvard Law Review* 4, no. 5. Retrieved April 11, 2014, from groups.csail.mit.edu/mac/classes/6.805/articles/privacy/Privacy_brand_warr2.html.

Woo, J. (2014, January 9). "*Foster v. Svenson*: When Privacy and Free Speech Collide." *Washington Lawyers for the Arts*. Retrieved April 15, 2014, from thewla.org/foster-v-svenson-when-privacy-and-free-speech-collide/.

Wood, D. (2003) "Albert Borgmann on Taming Technology: An Interview." *The Christian Century*. August 23: 22–25.

EIGHT

Serving the Market or the Marketplace?

The Business and Ethics of Social Media

Alan B. Albarran and Mitchell R. Haney

Social media is nothing short of a cultural revolution. In a relatively short amount of time, social networking sites have mushroomed in popularity both domestically and globally. Facebook has established itself as the leading social networking site in the world, and other sites have become leaders in their respective sub-markets of the social media industries. These include LinkedIn, a networking platform for professionals seeking employment; Twitter, the microblogging phenomenon that is known for users offering 140 character "tweets"; Instagram, where photographs are shared; and Pinterest, probably best described as an online scrapbooking site.

All of these leading social media entities engage millions of users, along with other sites like Google+, Groupon, Yelp, Foursquare, and Flickr, to name just a few. New startups are constantly entering the social media space to try and offer something unique to consumers. Snapchat is one such site that is generating a lot of interest—so much so that Facebook offered to buy the company for $3 billion in November 2013 (Rusli and MacMillan 2013). As society fully embraces mobile technology we can anticipate even more new entries trying to capture audiences.

Social media's growth as a business is also validated by the number of startups that have grown to become publicly traded companies. A publicly traded company carries more prestige than a non-public startup. A public company is in a better position to raise significant capital for future growth, and allows an opportunity for both institutional and "retail" (individual) investors to share in the potential growth of a company through appreciation and, where available, quarterly dividends. Linke- dIn and Groupon became public in 2011; Facebook and Yelp in 2012; Twitter became public in November 2013. Many of these sites were at- tractive to investors who gobbled up shares at their initial public offer- ings (IPO), sending valuations soaring. For example, Twitter's valuation on the first day of trading climbed to over $31 billion; it has since gone even higher (Seward 2013, November 7).

Further, investors recognize that social media companies are early in their development, with room for years of additional growth. While there is a lot the investment community is still learning about social media, one fact is evident: Social media sites are very popular with consumers. As such, advertisers have been flocking to social media sites to reach, in particular, mobile audiences.

THE POPULARITY OF SOCIAL MEDIA

According to the Pew Research Center, as of May 2013 approximately 72 percent of all adults in the United States use social media sites (Brenner 2013). A look at the statistics offered by Pew on its website illustrates that social media use is widespread, regardless of gender, ethnicity, or house- hold income. The data does show differentiation by age; younger adults (eighteen to twenty-nine) have the highest percentage of users (89 per- cent), followed by adults thirty to forty-nine (78 percent) and those aged fifty to sixty-four (60 percent). Older adults over sixty-five represent the lowest percentage of social media users (43 percent).

One key question for researchers: How much time are people spend- ing with social media? The amount of time varies depending on the source. For example, Ispos Open Thinking Exchange in January 2013 released data which suggested Americans spend three hours a day with social networking sites ("Social Networking Eats Up 3+ Hours Per Day" 2013). A United Press International story from June 2013 suggested social media usage averages twenty-three hours a week for adults, with young- er adults averaging twenty-eight hours a week (Survey: Americans spend 23 hours a week online/social media, 2013). A look at the Internet can find other data that suggests a range of from two to three and a half hours per day for most adults.

Clearly, social media penetration is high in the United States. Further, social media use is also capturing a lot of time among individuals, espe- cially those under the age of fifty. These factors have generated interest in social media beyond that of the audience and usage.

SOCIAL MEDIA AS AN ADVERTISING BUSINESS MODEL

The growth of social media sites, coupled with the data that confirms users are spending more and more time with social media, makes this nascent form of communication attractive to businesses seeking to tap in to an increasingly mobile, on-the-go audience. Advertisers and marketers covet the opportunity to reach consumers who are mobile, especially at the point of sale.

Traditional advertising in the form of newspapers, radio, and television cannot reach audiences at the exact point of sale like targeted advertising on mobile platforms. For decades, advertising on traditional media worked much like throwing darts at a dart board. Advertisers packaged messages in different program segments and day parts, hoping that the commercials might reach the desired target audience—and then hoping the audience might retain the message. Advertising in this manner is both inefficient and dependent on the recall level of the consumer.

Social media eliminates many of these inefficiencies. As consumers log in to various sites and "turn on" location services on their mobile devices, the GPS functionality can tell advertisers exactly where the consumer is and target messages aimed directly at that individual. Facebook and many other services like Foursquare and Yelp allow members to "check in" with their location, and even tell which "friends" are with them. This triggers potential offers to consumers at that location.

While these early location-based marketing efforts are somewhat crude, they will only become more sophisticated over time. As audience members "like" certain types of businesses, this information is shared with their own network. This exposure encourages other friends to "like" those same establishments, and increases awareness of offers available to the mobile audience.

The actual social media business model, as far as advertising is concerned, can be summed via the following points:

- Users establish profiles on different social media sites.
- Users invite friends/followers to join, creating a network of connections.
- Among the "data" on these profiles are many personal details about the individual and his or her connections.
- Advertisers buy messages to reach the users and their network of friends/followers.
- Users/friends/followers respond to advertising messages that interest them.
- The advertisers make money.
- The social media site, through advertising, makes money.
- The social media company grows with increased revenues and hopefully higher valuations.

If all of this seems farfetched, consider that as of December 2013, Facebook was estimated to have over 1.1 billion users, LinkedIn over 215 million, and Twitter around 200 million users. Advertisers access the many personal details and interests of users and their networks to create targeted advertising, with the goal of reaching the desired demographic with messages tailored just for their tastes and preferences.

MEETING MARKET EXPECTATIONS

From a business standpoint, social media holds unlimited potential as an advertising and marketing vehicle. As social media entities emerge to become publicly traded companies, shareholders and stakeholders expect their investment to appreciate over time and provide a reasonable rate of return. For those companies that remain private, investors provide startup capital and ongoing funds to cover operation costs until the firms are able to become profitable. The investors in privately held startups are also expecting a return on their investment.

These business factors have increased pressure on social media companies to increase revenues toward profitability. In this sense, social media companies are no different than any other business entities in that they have a profit-making orientation.

This has always created a paradox in capitalist-oriented societies as to the role of media. Should media companies serve the market (the actual users or customers if you want to think of it that way) or the marketplace (the advertisers and marketers)? Many companies claim they try to serve both the market and the marketplace—but it is difficult given the pressures associated with conducting business and the demands of stockholders and stakeholders.

One only has to look back in history to observe how economic pressures have changed the media over time. This topic is beyond the scope and purpose of this chapter, but deserves a couple of examples. The television networks have historically offered a nightly program schedule that appeals to women eighteen to forty-nine because females make most of the shopping decisions in households. Further, the "network model" for profitable programs now consists of a mix of comedies, a few dramas, and a lot of cheaply produced reality shows to reach audiences. Gone are the big-budget ensemble dramas, mini-series, documentaries, variety shows, westerns, and many other genres that were present only decades ago.

For news organizations, staffs have been reduced and some news bureaus shut down to increase profitability. News at the national and global level is now shared through the world's news agencies and pooled sources. Sports have been removed at most operations to save money, except for very local stories. Hours devoted to local newscasts have actually increased to reduce the marginal costs of presenting the news.

Social media companies are like traditional media companies in that they offer advertisers "access" to audiences. But social media is different in that now advertisers are equipped to leverage the intimacy associated with user profiles. Advertisers can now access not only the location of the user when made available, but a host of other specialized metrics to provide more targeted opportunities for marketers. Further, the size of each user's network of friends and followers allows for multiple "impressions" of an advertising message to be maximized to its fullest potential.

Companies outside of social media have been quick to jump on the growing bandwagon and join in the conversation. It is hard to find a business that does not have at minimum a Facebook page and at least one Twitter account; many firms have multiple pages and accounts. Businesses encourage users to "like" and "follow" them on social media sites, and this opens the door for the user to receive coupons, special offers, and other promotions. Plus, it encourages other users to sign on. For example, if I "like" ACME Hardware (a made-up business name as used here), and choose to "follow" the company via Twitter, then all of the people on my respective networks have the opportunity to be exposed to my activity. This may encourage others to follow/like ACME Hardware as well, which in turn allows their networks to be exposed to the same message.

A clear challenge for advertisers moving forward is finding the best methods to "mine" all of the data that social media generates every day about their campaigns, and then execute a strategy to utilize the data. Likewise, it is challenging for companies in the retail/services and other sectors to determine the best way to use the data available to them via friends and followers. Social media can be used to watch trends or "what is trending" in real time. The use of "hashtags" provides identifiers that can help locate activity using search engines. On Twitter "sponsored tweets" signify advertising messages; it is easy to then "retweet" the same message to a user's network of followers if desired. Social media can also be used to ferret out comments or tweets that are "unfavorable" to a business, allowing for quick and direct response to try and mitigate the impact of a negative posting.

The data analysis associated with social media is still in its infancy. More sophisticated tools and methods will enter the marketplace as companies learn the best way to manage and leverage the data generated across social media platforms. This is what makes social media so uniquely different from other traditional media platforms—the access to individual users and the access to networks and networks of friends.

AN ETHICAL TENSION IN THE SOCIAL MEDIA MARKETPLACE

The Tension

One ethical worry that arises, but is far from the only one, concerns the fact that one of the features so attractive to social media users is that they appear to be in control of a space which permits a unique, real-time expression of their individual beliefs, feelings, and interests. It is attractive to consumers, in part, because they appear to be able to have the autonomy of individual expression and free association in a medium that can be far-reaching and with immediacy. Users are attracted to the fact that they can also appreciate and respond to the personal expressions of others in their network, to those for whom they supposedly have some level of care or shared interests. Social media platforms provide a distinct sense of autonomy or control over individual expression similar to that found with face-to-face personal interactions between friends. Ironically, what attracts businesses to advertise through various social media platforms is both the sense of power and autonomy to control how they portray themselves as businesses, as well as to have access to more refined information for the targeting of their advertising messages.

The above culture of social media gives rise to an ethical tension which should be explored. As was raised earlier, can social network platforms serve both the consumer and the marketplace? As was also stated earlier, most traditional forms of media, such as television, newspapers, and magazines, claim to serve both. However, the push of business advertising has always been beset by the question of whether or not there is a kind of capturing of consumers without transparency and awareness. For instance, at the dawn of television, businesses sponsoring various early situation comedies, such as *The Honeymooners*, had direct input into the scripts so as to write story lines which promoted consumer behavior that was favorable to their industries. It was a kind of early product placement (of which many consumers are now much more aware), but actually it was a bit more insidious than just having a product in a scene in that the characters whom viewers came to love and identify with were written to role model behavior wanted by the industry (such as buying durable goods on credit) (French 1995, 46–56). The question of whether or not such use of media should raise concerns over a kind of deception that may undermine the autonomy of consumers remains. In marketing generally, there is a worry that marketers know more about the psychology of individuals' choices than do most consumers and that they use that knowledge to influence consumers into making economic decisions favorable to market actors.

What makes marketing in the space of social media have a potentially greater ethical tension than canonical media is that consumers are encouraged to actively express themselves in a candid manner and given the impression that the space is highly individualized and in their control, while at the same time it gives marketers even greater access to users' individual psychology to target business messages in more effective ways. This targeting is often done with less transparency to social media users because of what might be thought to be a milieu of personal autonomy. Certain populations, such as adolescents and children, those over the age of fifty who are not accustomed to social media, the undereducated, etc., may be even more vulnerable to marketing push than others in an arena that appears to them to be a free personal space for individual expression and personalized social connection with "friends."

The irony of social media as a business is that the more users express themselves the more social media can profit by selling that data or access to data to marketers in the attempt to push users buying habits in ways favorable to their clients. If anyone is skeptical of social media's ability to manipulate the psychology of its users, consider the following event. In January 2012, Facebook decided to see whether or not manipulating over 600,000 users' newsfeeds to only show positive stories or negative stories could alter their users' emotional states. They discovered that users' emotions could be manipulated without their knowledge or awareness, and they published the results of this "experiment" with a pair of university researchers in the Proceedings of the National Academy of Sciences in June 2014. (McNeal 2014) Much of the immediate discussion of this case has been over whether or not Facebook and the pair of researchers had met the standard of receiving Institutional Review Board approval which is a necessary ethical procedure for any academic research which involves human subjects. The core of why this ethical procedure is in place is to protect subjects from harm, including to protect subjects' autonomy. (Facebook argues that being a subject of research is part of the user agreement which all users "sign" when they establish their account.) What the study shows is that a social media business can use the medium of social media (in this case Facebook's newsfeed) to psychologically influence users without their being aware or noticing such influence (or being aware that Facebook had the inclination to dupe their users in such a manner). And, as was suggested above, part of what makes social media users problematically open to manipulation by market forces in this medium is precisely the sense that social media platforms are portrayed as spaces of personal autonomy.

Autonomy

To better understand the ethical tension here, a bit more should be said about the value of autonomy. In the thought of Immanuel Kant and Kantian inspired ethicists, as well as those in the rights tradition of ethics, autonomy figures as a feature of human beings which has significant moral relevance, if not overriding moral importance. In these traditions, human beings are never to be used as a mere means to one's own ends (Kant and Paton 1956). This entails that no agent may use another for their own gain while circumventing other's freedom or rationality. This tradition of thought is what undergirds all the work that has been done to ensure voluntary informed consent in areas like medicine and the law. And, in fact, voluntary informed consent is a value at the core of all business contractual relationships.

Autonomy is associated with the value of individual freedom. This is true, but what kind of freedom do we mean? Getting clear about this should help us deepen our appreciation of the kind of ethical tension that arises in social media businesses trying to serve two masters—the consumers and the market.

The often formulated basic kind of freedom that arises for almost all concerned with protecting human autonomy is freedom from interference. We see this in such ideas as the individual liberties protected by basic rights. These protections include freedom of expression, conscience, and privacy, among others. Freedom from interference is that we should not be impeded from acting in ways we want with the limitation that our acts should not impede others from doing the same. And often used conceptual elucidation of the protection from interference is that no person may use another without their expressed voluntary informed consent (Mappes 1992). There is also a more positive (although philosophically illusive) idea of freedom. This is the freedom to do as we wish. What makes this aspect of autonomy different from freedom from interference is that we can be free from impediment and yet never exercise the freedom to do what we wish. As such, there is an aspect of autonomy which is a freedom to believe, imagine, create, express, and so on. The respect for the autonomy of individuals often refers nebulously to a person both being free from unjustified restraint and to be able to think, be industrious, and express him or herself freely. Autonomy itself may be thought to be either valuable in itself or a necessary means to something else, like happiness or human flourishing, which is intrinsically valuable. Either way, autonomy, both in theory and in practice, has traditionally been held to be a core feature of moral living. If our theoretical and experiential insights into morality are correct, the manipulation by others that leads to the circumvention of either form of freedom captured under the value of autonomy constitutes to a moral wrong or harm. And, as such, if autonomy is thwarted, *prima facie*, there must be an overriding reason that explains why it is morally acceptable.

With this basic outline of the value of autonomy, and it is nothing but a rudimentary outline of some widely shared claims about its nature and value, we are in a better place to think more deeply about the ethical tension at the core of social media attempting to serve both consumers and the market. And it's a tension worth trying to understand and address given the ubiquitous use and market penetration of social media today.

The Analysis of the Ethical Tension

As was discussed earlier, social media companies are for-profit businesses that earn their wealth by providing access to its users and allowing advertisers much more nuanced access to target consumers based on data provided by the users themselves. The general question that arises is whether or not the collection of individual information about users' interests, desires, connections, etc., and that users provide in their free acts of individual expression, should be used to tailor the push of advertising information toward said users and to even manipulate what is highlighted in users' networks, constitutes a problematic violation of users' autonomy? Does it constitute social media and marketers treating users as mere means to their own ends or violating voluntary informed consent?

How might it be that social media companies and their business clients may actually be violating the autonomy of its users? Well, there are a few interconnected ways in which autonomy of individual users may be threatened.

1. Social media companies and marketers use information, even information which users believe they have locked down to just their circle of friends, to help develop a consumer profile of users but in a space whose attraction is the feel of distinctly interpersonal communication (rather than public or mass communication).
2. Social media businesses encourage a climate of users expressing themselves as much as possible. They encourage a climate of sharing, not primarily to promote better relationships and connections between users but to glean people's information for the purpose of having clearer and more accurate market data to sell to existing and potential advertisers (or they allow third-party companies to cull that data).
3. Social media businesses typically only meet the legal minimum in an attempt to ensure that their users are well-informed of their data use policies (that is, they do a minimal job in ensuring users are aware and understand that all their information is being culled for the purpose of creating sellable profiles to advertisers).

If any of the above worries are true, then there is some concern that user autonomy is threatened, if not violated, within the present structure of social media in its attempt to serve both masters. And the first two worries are interconnected in intimate ways.

Social media spaces are a mongrel space of communication. Users are generally aware that the platforms are publicly accessible or open in

many ways, if for no other reason than the multitude of stories of personal embarrassment shared by word of mouth or covered by more traditional news media. However, the nature and structure of the communication has developed a culture closer to that of informal, interpersonal communication. People are generally very informal in their use of social media. They use slang and emoticons throughout many things they share.
Users post jokes, memes, idiosyncratic ideas, or even personal confes-
sions that they may not share in "polite company." Social media has the
distinct feel of informal, interpersonal communication, but it also has the
effect associated with the feel of anonymity or privacy from behind the
keyboard or smart phone. It is this milieu of interpersonal communication which social media companies want to foster.

It is through users feeling comfortable to share, like, make connections, and express their personal lives at-will that social media companies
(as well as third-party companies) can best sell highly individualized
market data so as to push various products and services directly to individual users who fit a unique profile. Through users "letting-their-
guards-down" and expressing without the kind of censure that may
come in more formal, public atmospheres of communication, social media provides marketers access to information about consumers that they
may have difficulty culling through other means. Thus, social media
companies use the apparent positive freedom of users (their freedom to
express) to benefit themselves.

There is a worry, as a result of the above, that social media companies
and their advertising clients want social media space to feel as if it is
protected from the disclosure of personal information (for example, likes,
desires, ideas, attractions, and so on) because they want access to those
personal expressions that users may not share in more public settings
(such as market surveys or focus groups). They encourage and allow to
spread virally through the online culture the idea that social media platforms are a protected and unimpeded space of private, interpersonal
communication and expression. In a sense it is true that users are free to
think, create, express, and whatnot. But it's under the impression that
social media space is a kind of protected, private space for such use of
one's freedom. For social media business to encourage and not readily
correct the impression that it is a safe space for open personal expression
is a form of deception. It is a deception by way of letting misconceptions
or an inappropriate understanding of the circumstances stand when it
serves your purposes. If this is the case, then social media companies and
marketers are potentially undermining the autonomy of the users. They
are clearly at risk of treating users as mere means to their own ends
because users are divulging information under an easily corrected misconception that social media is generally a protected space to disclose
intimate, personal information without it being used against them (at
least not used against them by parties unknown to the user).

Social media companies argue that they have user agreements that all users must acknowledge and consent to in the process of establishing their accounts (and acknowledge any changes made after having an account). The industry argues that this constitutes the fulfillment of voluntary informed consent undergirded by the moral value of respect for autonomy. Granted, the formal acknowledgment by a user constitutes having met the legal standard of acceptance, and a minimal procedural standard of voluntary informed consent.

In the arena of bioethics we find a mature and developed discussion of what is required to meet voluntary informed consent in order to protect the autonomy of patients. Many bioethicists agree that there is much more to meeting the standard of voluntary informed consent than found in people acknowledging that they are aware of or even said they have read a policy statement and that they have signed it (see Applebaum et al. 1987). The important elements from the point of view of the protection of autonomy are that the user knows concrete as well as general details of what they are committing themselves to in terms that they can understand. The problem is that many user agreements are articulated in ways that have a number of disadvantages to ensuring knowledge of the terms at the user's level of understanding. A first issue is that user agreements are often written as legal contracts in the terms of contract law which means you need to be a trained lawyer or very well educated to understand the nature of the agreement. This is an impediment to the vast majority of users genuinely giving voluntary informed consent because they may not understand the agreement even if they pass their eyes over the entire contract. For social media businesses to simply say that its users' responsibility to understand the contract abdicates a responsibility that agents' have to others to be clear as to terms of any agreement in projects that require joint contributions.

In response to such a worry Facebook, for instance, has developed pages dedicated to explaining the terms of their user agreement including how users' data will and will not be used. Their pages do avoid the use of clearly legal jargon. However, to fully grasp the implications one would have to devote a fairly substantial amount of time to reading the multiple pages and subpages dedicated to explaining what is and is not involved in the legal version of the user agreement. Social media companies (and businesses in general) know that if any task is thought to be too time consuming, even if it is not in legal terminology and construction, most consumers will not dedicate the time necessary to understand the conditions before signing the user agreement. In addition, the language is used in these explanatory pages is still pretty advanced, and they likely require an advanced college level reading ability to understand. As such, there is the appearance of attempting to have users understand the nature of their policies regarding personal data, but it still tends to undermine voluntary informed consent for all but a relatively narrow class of educated, cautious, and inquisitive persons. Finally, in the case of voluntary informed consent in medicine, the gold standard of meeting the standard is to have patients explain what they are agreeing to in their own words. This is a final measure to ensure by the medical staff that the patient adequately understands that to which he or she is agreeing. Social media businesses (and businesses in general) have no set expectation to attempt to elicit from users evidence that users adequately understand that to which they are contractually committing themselves. Given these obstacles, the measures that social media businesses argue meet the protection of user autonomy from violation are dubious. It appears that social media businesses at this point largely do not make a good faith effort to ensure the autonomy of their users and do so by in large only at the level of the legal minimum rather than the moral optimum. Thus, most users are likely unaware of that to which they are agreeing in the use of their personal information, and social media providers are typically not encouraging understanding by users of their policies concerning how their personal information and data will be used.

CONCLUSION

If any of the above concerns are reasonable, then social media businesses and their advertising clients are jeopardizing the autonomy of persons who use social media platforms. In the attempt to serve two masters—consumers and the market—social media businesses risk failing consumers for the benefit of themselves and their advertisers. They do so by taking users' acts of positive freedom for the purpose of possible manipulation for their own ends without having clearly and completely met the standard of voluntary informed consent required by protection from interference. Does this mean it is an impossible task to both economically benefit from delivery of service and to morally protect the autonomy of users? It is not, but, at present, social media companies are falling short of meeting the second demand.

A few solutions present themselves as reasonable answers to this ethical tension. First, social media could charge users directly for access to their platforms and not rely on the sales of advertising. However, this would likely lead to a steep drop in use as many people may not be able to afford pay-to-use services in the realm of social media. And there are benefits from access to the real-time communication platform of social media for those who lack access to other forms of media. One need only think of the use of social media in the Arab Spring to see how this can be the case. Second, social media businesses can protect the data of users such that advertising is no more targeted than the general demographics one finds in more traditional media. However, this threatens to undermine revenues for social media businesses, unless access to more than a billion users is still worthwhile to advertisers even when they cannot capture very narrow segments of the consumer market. Nevertheless, if revenues drop, this may make advertising via social media no more attractive than say television and likely curtail revenue for social media businesses and place pressure on them to begin to charge for services. Thus, it would return us to issues raised in the first solution. Third, and finally, social media businesses could possibly better protect user autonomy through two measures: a) Being proactive in making user agreements much more clear and transparent to individual users (as well as when they make changes to user agreements); and b) developing or supporting educational programs about the nature and use of social media.

If social media businesses want to meet the protection of autonomy of users, then they should make a good faith effort to explain to a variety of types of users, including adolescents, the under-educated, and to those who are new to social media culture. They should engage educators in how to best educate users about the standards of data use they employ and to what extent data is used to build profiles in order to push advertising at a user. They could consult educators to aid in both how to educate individual users who are considering signing up for their services, as well as educating the wider culture about the nature of their businesses, how users can protect information they don't want third parties having access to, and so on. Thus, they could proactively take good faith measures to protect the autonomy of consumers both at individual consumers and consumer culture at large. It is true that some potential users will be reluctant to use their social media once they understand the nature of the business model, but for many who are already aware of its nature, they still have chosen to utilize the kind of communication platforms offered by social media to make connections, express their interests, and add it to other ways in which they add value to their lives. However, if social media businesses acted more transparently and with active attempts to make sure users and the general population were informed of the nature of their business and its services, then they would be in a better position, ethically speaking, in preserving the important and widely acknowledged value of autonomy.

REFERENCES

Albarran, A. B. (2013). *The Social Media Industries*. New York: Routledge.

Appelbaum, P. S., Roth, L. H., Lidz, C. W., Benson, P., and W. Winslade. (1987). "False hopes and best data: Consent to research and the therapeutic misconception." *The Hastings Center Report* 17 (2): 20–24.

Brenner, J. (2013). Pew Internet: Social Networking (full detail). Retrieved November 14, 2013 from pewinternet.org/Commentary/2012/March/Pew-Internet-Social-Networking-full-detail.aspx.

French, P. (1995) Corporate Ethics. Fort Worth: Harcourt Brace.

Kant, I., and H. J. Paton. (1956). *The Moral Law: Kant's Groundwork of the Metaphysic of Morals*. London: Hutchinson University Library.

Mappes, T. (1992). "Sexual morality and the concept of using another person." In Thomas Mappes and Jane Zembaty, eds., *Social Ethics*, 4th edition. New York: McGraw-Hill. 203–26.

McNeal, G. *Forbes Magazine OnLine*. Retrieved July 1, 2014 from www.forbes.com/sites/gregorymcneal/2014/06/28/facebook-manipulated-user-news-feeds-to-create-emotional-contagion/.

Rusli, E. M., and D. MacMillan. (2013, November 13). "Snapchat Spurned $3 Billion Acquisition Offer from Facebook." Retrieved November 15, 2013 from blogs.wsj.com/digits/2013/11/13/snapchat-spurned-3-billion-acquisition-offer-from-facebook/.

Seward, Z. M. (2013, November 7). "Twitter Starts Trading at an Astounding Valuation of $31.3 Billion." Retrieved November 28, 2013 from qz.com/144720/twitter-starts-trading-at-an-astounding-valuation-of-31-3-billion/.

"Social Networking Eats Up 3+ Hours Per Day for the Average American User." Retrieved November 14, 2013 from www.marketingcharts.com/wp/interactive/social-networking-eats-up-3-hours-per-day-for-the-average-american-user-26049/.

Survey: Americans spend 23 hours a week online/social media. Retrieved November 14, 2013 from www.upi.com/Science_News/Technology/2013/06/29/Survey-Americans-spend-23-hours-a-week-onlinesocial-media/UPI-61961372562999/.

NINE

Perspectives from China

Social Media and Living Well in a Chinese Context

Sarah Mattice

The United States has a current population of approximately 313.9 million people. In 2013, more than 600 million users had active accounts on Qzone, China's largest social media site (Millward 2013). Although discussions of social media tend to assume American or European users, social media is a worldwide phenomenon, and different locales bring different concerns to bear on social media ethics.[1] China not only leads the world in terms of sheer numbers of users, but also has the most active environment for social media, ranging from instant chat platforms like QQ to blogs, microblogs, social networking sites, and gaming platforms. Chinese users also spend approximately 40 percent of their time online on social media sites (Chiu, Ip, and Silverman 2012). Given this, inquiries into social media ethics should involve China (and other non-Anglo-European locales and concerns). This chapter is split into two parts: part I draws on distinctly Chinese philosophical conceptions of living well in order to provide a cultural recontextualization of some of the questions associated with social media and ethical development, and to hopefully enrich larger discussions of social media ethics; part II considers the contemporary situation of social media in China, what social media actually looks like in China, and some of the political concerns surrounding social media in China.

CHINESE CONCEPTIONS OF THE GOOD LIFE AND SOCIAL MEDIA

The Chinese philosophical landscape is relevantly different from western philosophical landscapes in a variety of ways, and so to consider the distinctly Chinese ethical concerns that arise from social media requires brief discussions of accounts of living well in the three most prominent religio-philosophical traditions in China: Confucianism, Daoism, and Buddhism. Although ancient, each of these traditions is a key thread in the complex interweaving of contemporary China's ethical fabric. As will be seen from what follows, none of these traditions seem to provide a hard-and-fast rule about whether or not social media usage coincides with the visions of living well they present. Although on the one hand this may simply be because social media is a relatively new phenomenon, there is a deeper reason for the lack of a firm answer. These three traditions are not principle-based ethical systems that provide a decision procedure for determining best actions. Unlike some versions of consequentialism or deontology, neither Confucianism, Daoism, nor Chinese Buddhism are particularly interested in establishing a set of rules from which all good conduct can be deduced. In addition, these traditions tend to focus on practices, habits, and events, and so rather than "the good life" the phrase "living well" is more apt. Even the Buddhist paramitas, which include the five lay precepts, serve more as guidelines for compassionate and wise action and intentions than strict rules to be followed. Instead, these traditions focus on providing concrete visions of living well in particular circumstances, and call for moral imagination in responding to the unknown. In each tradition, the vision of living well is made concrete through an ethical exemplar: the Confucian exemplary person (*junzi*), the Daoist sage (*shengren*), and the Buddhist bodhisattva (*pusa*). The following sections use these figures to orient the discussion of Chinese philosophical perspectives on the ethics of social media.

Confucianism (Exemplary Persons)

Confucianism is a religio-philosophical tradition indigenous to China that traces its lineage to Kongzi (Confucius 551–479 BCE), who lived and taught during the end of the Spring and Autumn Period.[2] It developed during the Warring States Period with teachers such as Mengzi (Mencius) and Xunzi, and after its adoption as state ideology during the Han Dynasty, spread across much of East Asia. Indeed, as Roger Ames and Henry Rosemont Jr. (1998) state, "whatever we might mean by 'Chineseness' today, some two and a half millennia after his death, is inseparable from the example of personal character that Confucius provided for posterity" (1).

Early Confucian philosophy understands the world in terms of a person-centered hierarchy, where all relations are, in a sense, power relations, and both the root and the flowering of human experience is in personal, and especially familial, relationships. As French sinologist Marcel Granet notes, "Chinese wisdom had no need of the idea of God," and indeed much early Confucian thought was structured around this world and our roles and relations in it (1934). Persons are understood neither as radically autonomous nor as soul-bearers, but as constitutively relational; persons are no more and no less than the sum of their roles and relationships. Confucian ethics is deeply intertwined with political concerns, as the period in which Confucian thought developed was one of incessant internecine warfare, and Confucius himself sought a political appointment in order to influence a regent and help to bring order to an age of brutality. Although he was ultimately unsuccessful as a minister, as a teacher he was incredibly influential.

Confucian ethics is, broadly speaking, a project of self-cultivation, refinement, and attention to roles and relationships, and an ideal at the heart of this ethical vision is the *junzi*, the exemplary person. Exemplary persons are characterized by their humaneness (*ren*), their attention to good form and ritual propriety (*li*), their appropriateness and emphasis on moral cultivation over profit (*yi*), and their wisdom and practical understanding (*zhi*). Much of the text of the *Analects* consists in short conversations between Confucius and his students, his students and their students, and passages detailing Confucius as a moral exemplar in his daily life. The *Analects* has many passages concerned with exemplary persons as moral ideals: they are not mere vessels (2.12); they first accomplish what they are going to say, and only then say it (2.13); they cherish excellence and fairness (4.11); they are neither bent on nor against anything, but go with what is appropriate (4.10); they do not leave off of humaneness for even the space of a meal (4.5); they learn broadly of culture, discipline this learning through ritual propriety, and can remain on course without straying from it (6.27) (*Analects*, trans. Ames and Rosemont Jr. 1998).

In today's world, which is in many ways far removed from Warring States China, how might we understand the relationship between a Confucian project of self-cultivation and participating in social media? While Confucianism is an ancient tradition, it continues to animate contemporary Chinese concerns in a variety of ways. Mary Bockover, in her article "Confucian Values and the Internet" argues that Confucian values—still flourishing in today's world—are in many ways inconsistent with core values of the internet such as liberal freedoms and democracy of information. She writes that "The Internet is currently the most effective form of communication available to promote the first-world value of autonomy: It is driven by the ideas of consumerism, free expression, equal opportunity, and free trade. This stands in sharp moral contrast to the traditional Confucian system of values" (2003, 164). Bockover draws on early Confucian philosophy and emphasizes that Confucian values such as *ren* (humaneness) and *xiao* (familiality, family reverence) entail a set of cultural priorities that does not include any particular interest in western liberal values: "the moral priority of Confucian ethics is to cultivate and fulfill one's social responsibilities. To reconcile one's obligations to others is the most pressing concern, not to be a 'self,' or a person *qua* autonomous or 'free' agent in any sense" (2003, 163). Her argument rests on a pair of claims: first, it is not at all clear that contemporary American definitions of freedom as unobstructed self-expression are either the only or the best definitions of freedom, and so to suggest that Confucian philosophy might have legitimate interests and values that conflict with that notion of freedom is certainly possible; and second, given that China has never strongly embraced or practiced unrestricted liberty, it is culturally imperialistic to suggest that they should with regard to the internet simply because westerners do, even with all of the problems that have come with the internet. It is reasonable to suggest that China might look to Confucian philosophy to articulate its own set of priorities that may not include unrestricted autonomy on the internet.

Wong Pak-hang agrees with Bockover, although for different reasons. He narrows his focus to social media, and argues that there are three characteristics of social media that do not resonate well with Confucian ethics: invisible audiences, collapsed contexts, and the blurring of public and private (Wong 2013). Like Bockover, he situates his discussion of Confucian ethics in terms of the special significance of familial relationships, social roles, and ritual activity (*li*) for living well in a Confucian context. He argues that "whether social media is desirable or not depends first and foremost on its impact on roles," and most importantly its impact on familial roles and relationships (Wong 2013, 289). Considering the problems of invisible audiences and collapsed contexts—it is often the case that one's audience on social media is not actively present, may be anonymous, and may collapse relevantly different contexts down into one online realm—Wong argues that not knowing whom one is addressing is, from a Confucian perspective, a serious problem. Confucian ethics places great emphasis on social roles and relationships as constitutive of one's personhood, and also on ritual activity and propriety as a way of organizing and structuring one's interactions. Not knowing whom one is addressing makes it extremely difficult to know how to act well, from a Confucian perspective: we speak and act differently when with family, friends, employers, strangers, and so on. The blurring of public and private that often happens online de-prioritizes the family, and Confucian ethics requires a strong family as the foundation for moral growth. Wong thus concludes that Confucians will ultimately find social media undesirable, although he opens the door for possible social and/or technological innovation that might challenge this.

Both of these thinkers suggest, in general, that engaging in social media is difficult to do as part of Confucian project. There may, however, be some ways in which we could understand the drive to become an exemplary person (*junzi*) as benefited by social media. Confucian ethics is often described as a project of growth in relationships, and participation in social media does offer certain avenues for growth in relationships that may be unavailable offline. Platforms such as Facebook and Twitter offer the possibility of establishing and maintaining connections with people who may be distant. They may not be the only way of doing this, but they certainly are well set up to facilitate connections. The extent to which these connections are genuine relationships in a fully Confucian sense is unclear, but as exemplary persons do tend to gather others around them, social media sites are possible loci for keeping up these connections when in-person meetings are not possible (assuming that Confucians would prefer face-to-face contact, which seems unproblematic).

In addition to maintaining long-distance relationships, social media is often used for some level of political engagement. From a Confucian perspective, part of what makes the *junzi* an exemplar is that the moral and political realms are understood to be inseparable. Self-cultivation is a political project, and as such political engagement is an important dimension of living well for Confucians.[3] In a political environment such as China where direct engagement and remonstration may be difficult or dangerous, engagement through anonymous microblogging sites allows for political participation that otherwise might not be possible. There are obvious comparisons here with the activity of the Arab Spring, where social media served an important role in part because open discussion was prohibited.[4]

Finally, engagement with social media may blur the lines between public and private in potentially helpful ways. Although Wong's concern about the loss of emphasis on the familial realm is a live issue, with skillful engagement social media could draw attention to the increasing accuracy of the Confucian claim that the boundary between public and private is thin at best, and serve to draw attention and focus to the performative aspects of living well, and the need for managing all of one's interactions in an exemplary way. In a world where opting out of the online is increasingly difficult, engagement with social media can draw attention to persons as relationally constituted, and also highlight the flow of power between people (*guanxi*).

Although there may be some possibilities for convergence between a Confucian project of living well and social media, we can build on some of the critical resources offered by Bockover and Wong to suggest additional concerns. First, one of the persistent concerns of early Confucian thought is the idea that *how* one acts is as important as *what* one does—style and substance are ethically intertwined: "Zixia asked about filial conduct. The Master replied: 'It all lies in showing the proper countenance. As for the young contributing their energies when there is work to be done, and deferring to their elders when there is wine and food to be had—how can merely doing this be considered being filial?" (*Analects* 2.8, 1988, 78). It is not simply that the young should defer to the old, but *how* they defer that really matters. The Confucian exemplary person is refined and cultured, and demonstrates this in the success with which she navigates the variety of relationships and roles that constitute her. Unfortunately, refined and cultured speech are not the norm on most social media sites, and few actively promote a care for the links between speech and action that a Confucian perspective values.

Second, part of a Confucian project of living well is emulating and coming to embody moral exemplars. Because social media is, relatively speaking, a new phenomenon, identifying social media exemplars who fully embody the *junzi* ideal is challenging, to say the least. As a new arena of life, we lack the generations of cultural resources available for judging moral exemplars in face-to-face realms. And because many people spend large chunks of time online and on social media platforms, the people they choose to emulate and raise up as exemplars are especially important—many spend more time on social media than in face-to-face engagement, and so figuring out how to find good role models online is crucial. In *Analects* 4.1, Confucius says, "In taking up one's residence, it is the presence of humane persons (*ren*) that is the greatest attraction. How can anyone be called wise who, in having the choice, does not seek to dwell among humane people?" (89, "humane" substituted for "authoritative"). As relationally constituted persons, the moral character and quality of those with whom we enter into relationships and spend time is crucial to our own moral development. The people we spend time with become part of ourselves, and as such, the skill to judge who to spend time with is particularly important to our ethical cultivation.

Related to the issue of identifying moral exemplars online, one of the most serious concerns raised by a Confucian account of living well regarding social media has to do with children. In contrast to much of western philosophy, Confucian philosophy is explicitly concerned with education and with the development of children into adults. In fact, some describe Confucianism as first and foremost a philosophy of education. Living well is not only about oneself, but about one's family, friends, and broader community as they extend from the distant cultural past through us into the next generations. The impact of social media usage on children and their moral development, then, is a central concern raised by Confucianism.

Consider, for instance, a connection we might make between *Mengzi* 1A7 and a recent performance by American comedian Louis C. K. *Mengzi* 1A7 is a conversation between Mengzi and King Xuan of Qi, concerning the moral qualities relevant to good leadership. Mengzi tells the king that he heard a story of the king seeing an ox being led to ritual slaughter and pardoning it. Mengzi draws this out to suggest that the king, in responding to the suffering of the ox in front of him, has the seeds from which to develop a moral heart. One of the keys of developing morally in Confucian thought is the idea of face, and of shame. Being confronted in person with the ox, and sparing it, demonstrates to Mengzi that the king is capable of being a humane leader (although he has failed to do so). His failure is a matter of effort, not of impossibility.

In an interview on the late night talk show *Conan*, Louis C. K. discusses why he does not want his children to have cell phones (and specifically constant access to mobile social media), showing a very Mengzian kind of concern for the ways in which online interaction leaves an important hole in children's moral development. He says,

> I'm not raising children, I'm raising the grownups they are going to be. . . . Kids are mean, and it's because they're trying it out. They look at a kid and go "You're fat!" and then they see the kid's face scrunch up and they say, it doesn't feel good to make a person do that. But they have to start with doing the mean thing [and seeing the result]. But when they write [online] "You're fat!" they go "mmm that was fun, I like that." (teamcoco.com 2013)[5]

Although he is making a comedic performance, his words resonate with the *Mengzi*, and the concern that personal interaction is an important component of moral development, most especially for children. Social media, then, can be a hindrance to moral development in that it is often a substitute for the face-to-face interaction necessary for cultivating both empathy and shame, key features of the development into a *junzi*.

Given a Confucian account of moral development and the ethical exemplar of the *junzi*, the exemplary person, it would seem that social media is at best an add-on for social interaction, and at worst a genuine obstacle to self-cultivation and the life of a *junzi*. There is a sense in which the possibilities for productive engagement with social media are not so much for one who is trying to live well and become a *junzi*, but perhaps for one who is already exemplary, social media may be able to serve these potentially beneficial functions. From a Confucian perspective, for those whose moral development is still inchoate, however, and especially for children, the dangers of social media for living well are substantial.

Daoism (Sages)

Daoism, like Confucianism, is a religio-philosophical tradition that traces its lineage back to the Spring and Autumn Period and the Warring States Period of early China. Two of the most important early figures associated with philosophical Daoism are Laozi and the text the *Daodejing*, and Zhuang Zhou and the *Zhuangzi*.[6] Although Daoism and Confucianism share a cosmological foundation that arises out of the *Yijing* (*Book of Changes*), which is fundamentally this-world oriented, and focuses on patterns of change and persistence, unlike Confucianism Daoism extends

its focus from personal relationships to the natural world. Daoist philosophy also places great emphasis on cultivating certain kinds of productive
dispositions to most effectively and playfully navigate the world.[7] The
name "Daoism" (*Daojia/Daojiao*) comes from the term *dao*, which is one of
the most rich and difficult terms in all of Chinese intellectual history.[8] Its
meanings can range from road(s) or path(s) to the activity of making
road(s)/path(s); from the way(s) to do something to prescriptive discourse about how best to do something; all the way to the energizing
process that is the dynamic dance of the cosmoi. Much of Daoist philosophy is concerned with questions of how to find and best travel along/
with *dao*.

One Daoist ethical exemplar is the *shengren*, or sage, who is often
depicted as living a simple but aesthetically rich life. In the *Dao De Jing*
there are many passages that describe sages: sages practice emptiness
(11), preserve the female and are *yin*, pliable, and supple (28, 76), and
they live naturally and free from desires, recognitions, and standards
given in human distinctions (37). They settle down and know how to be
content (46), act with no expectation of reward (2, 51), never make a
display of themselves (22, 24, 72), and do not linger to receive praise (77);
they manifest plainness and simplicity, never thinking only of themselves, they create peace (32) and cause no injury (60) (*Dao De Jing*, trans.
Ames and Hall 2003). Sages are ideals of living well in moral, political,
and aesthetic dimensions of life.

Although there is not much scholarly attention to possible relations
between Daoist philosophy and contemporary social media, we can identify some ways in which there might be beneficial interaction, and some
in which engagement with social media might be detrimental to Daoist
projects. One of the common Daoist critiques of their Confucian counter-
parts is that the Confucians have an undesirable tendency to reify social
roles and to become dogmatically attached to ritual activity. As mentioned in the previous section, for Confucians the fact that social media
can make it difficult to maintain social boundaries is undesirable. From a
Daoist perspective, however, the potential openness and interaction
across social boundaries offered by social media could be a good thing,
and help to maintain awareness that social status is a matter of conven-
tion. When even Confucius wants the man with the chopped foot as his
teacher, this reversal, and the reversal of other assumptions about conventional understanding, indicates the importance of crossing conventional boundaries.[9]

In addition, Daoists are often critical of the rigidity of common morality. They instead advocate a playful, open, and flexible response to the
changes of the world. We can imagine, then, that one Daoist response to
social media might be wonder and amusement at this new development
the world has to offer. After all, Master Yu responded with joy at the
prospect of having his left arm turned into a rooster and his right into a

crossbow![10] Daoism might in fact offer a valuable perspective on an element of social media that is often criticized today: Many people get much of their news from social media, and fall into the pattern of seeing only the kinds of things that they agree with. In suggesting that sages cultivate the productive emptiness of a bellows or the open center of a wheel, a Daoist might value the online availability of differing perspectives. Daoist philosophy tends to be critical of perspectives that think they have the entire picture and are unable or unwilling to adopt a sense that their perspective is one of many possible perspectives. The *Zhuangzi* advocates understanding perspective as a kind of lodging place, and in the opening image of the Peng bird (a bird so large that flapping its wings causes seasonal change), suggests that adopting a kind of epistemological capaciousness is a valuable strategy. Being able to access many different kinds of perspectives online, then, could be extremely valuable—although one would have to go to the effort of doing so.

Furthermore, the Daoist sage is often depicted as a master of immediacy: "Sages really think and feel immediately" (*Dao De Jing* 49, 153). They are often compared with infants, in that infants respond in the moment, without calculation or deception. Chapter 10 of the *Dao De Jing* asks, "In concentrating your *qi* and making it pliant, / Are you able to become the newborn babe?" and Chapter 55 opens by saying that "One who is vital in character (*de*) / Can be compared with a newborn babe" (*Dao De Jing*, Ames and Hall 2003). One of the commonalities among social media platforms is their brevity and immediacy. Twitter and platforms like it allow only a limited number of characters, and saying something in that way can truly be an exercise in spontaneity.

Not only do Daoists value spontaneity in the sense of the immediacy of the infant or the potency of the child, but they also value spontaneity in the sense of the ability to act without detailed consideration made possible by extensive practice—a jazz musician who can improvise brilliantly because of years of dedication. Furthermore, in a Daoist philosophy of language, language is seen as provisional but effective, and at its best when it poetically opens up a world rather than discursively closes it down: "naming (*ming*) that can assign fixed reference to things is not really naming" (*Dao De Jing* 1, Ames and Hall 2003). Daoists are wary of definitions but love metaphors, and so the brevity inherent in certain social media platforms could provide a useful outlet for cultivating these aspects of sagacity. Ames and Hall write that for Daoists, the "locus of sagacious thinking lies in inspiring and transforming the ordinary and routine business of the common people . . . sagacious living in drawing together and focusing the aspirations of the community" (154). Platforms like Twitter certainly involve the "ordinary," the "routine," and bringing a community together, and a Daoist on the path to becoming a sage might take the opportunity to use it as a means of development.

However, in other ways it is difficult to see living well in a Daoist fashion coinciding with much social media usage. Daoist philosophy generally advocates living simply, naturally, and without artifice; social media is in some respects an unnatural complication that introduces a variety of artifice into living. Chapter 19 of the *Dao De Jing* exhorts readers to "Display a genuineness like raw silk and embrace a simplicity like unworked wood," (104) and Chapter 47 states, "Venture not beyond your doors to know the world. . . . The farther one goes the less one knows" (150). Daoist values often lean toward simplicity, reserve, and locality; social media does not seem to resonate much with those values.

A great deal of Daoist poetry and prose is connected with the ideal of the Daoist sage as a hermit, one who is critical of popular social practices, has renounced life at court, and who retreats to the forests or mountains to live simply with nature. Tao Yuanming's *Peach Blossom Spring* (*Tao Hua Yuan Ji*) is a widely influential Daoist story from 421CE that tells of the journey of a fisherman to a chance discovery of an idyllic village untouched by the "modern" world. The way in which this story, and others like it, valorizes the simple, natural life seems at odds with the contemporary conveniences and contrivances of social media.

In addition to living the life of a recluse, the Daoist sage is sometimes understood as a kind of artist who turns her life into a work of art. Early Daoist texts often praise and value the time and effort required to become really good at something, especially something that contributes beauty to the culture. Many famous Daoists were artists—poets, writers, calligraphers, painters, and musicians—and the dedication to their art is especially prized as a major component of living well. While social media engagement may not prevent this dedication, people who are active on social media often spend huge chunks of time online. This is time that then cannot generally be devoted to aesthetic cultivation or training.[11]

Buddhism (Bodhisattvas)

> Why doesn't the Buddha have a Facebook profile pic?
> Because there are no selfies![12]

Buddhism is a set of religio-philosophical traditions that originated with the historical figure of Siddharta Gautama and his articulation of the Four Noble Truths in approximately the sixth-fifth centuries BCE, in the region of the world that is now Nepal/India.[13] Buddhist traditions moved to China sometime around the first century CE, took root during the Three Dynasties period after the fall of the Han, and flourished during the Tang Dynasty. Buddhist accounts of living well begin with the Four Noble Truths:

1. All this is suffering/unsatisfactoriness.
2. There is a pattern in how suffering arises.

3. There is a pattern in how suffering is resolved.
4. There is an Eightfold Path for turning suffering toward meaningful resolution: right view, right intention, right speech, right action, right livelihood, right effort, right mindfulness, and right concentration.[14]

Living well, then, requires recognizing the sources of one's suffering and changing how one lives so as to decrease/eliminate suffering in one's own life and in the lives of others through interconnected practices of wisdom (right view and intention), morality (right speech, action, and livelihood), and meditation (right effort, mindfulness, and concentration).

Suffering is said to be caused in part by three poisons: attachment, aversion, and ignorance. One of the major causes of suffering is the three poisons in relation to the idea of a permanent, unchanging, essential self (*atman*). It is through our attachment to this fiction, our ignorance of how things really are (impermanent, changing, and non-substantial), and our aversion to pain, suffering, and death that many of our problems arise.

Many of the Buddhist traditions in China are Mahayana Buddhist traditions, which take as their ideal the figure of the Bodhisattva, one who vows out of compassion to remain in the cycles of birth and death to attend to the suffering of all sentient beings. Guanyin is one of the most famous and important Bodhisattvas in China, and she is often depicted with one thousand (many) arms, symbolic of her pledge to compassionately respond to the suffering of all sentient beings. There are many different schools of Chinese Buddhism, all of which draw their lineage back through different Indian Buddhist schools to the historical Buddha. Some of the most prominent schools are: Three Treatise (*San Lun*), Consciousness-only (*Wei Shi*), Tian Tai, Pure Land (*Jing Tu*), Flower Garland (*Hua Yan*), and Chan.[15] As mentioned earlier, most of these schools fall into the general family of Mahayana Buddhism (the greater vehicle), as distinct from Theravada Buddhism (the way of the elders) and Vajrayana Buddhism (the diamond vehicle).[16] For the sake of brevity, much of what follows draws on a specifically Chan philosophical perspective, as Chan is a distinctly Chinese school of Buddhism: "The Chinese sense of wisdom colors Chan" (Jun 2013, 29).[17]

In Mahayana Buddhism the image of the Bodhisattva serves to establish a family of teachings that illustrate a life of service to others, based on an understanding and lived realization of co-dependent origination, emptiness of self, compassion, and wisdom. Characteristic of Bodhisattva teachings are the six paramitas: generosity, discipline, patience, energy, contemplation, and wisdom. These paramitas, or perfections, are qualities of cultivation required for the Bodhisattva path; they are interconnected and interdependent. The second paramita, living in a disciplined manner, includes at least the five lay precepts: no intentional killing, no lying, no sexual misconduct, no stealing, and no intoxication. These precepts point to important behaviors to avoid if one wants to live well: "Practice is . . . about crafting the art of living beautifully, honestly, and with strength and dignity. Precepts are a refinement of this craft; they are a mindfulness tool and a tool of compassion that can open body, speech, and mind to original wholesomeness" (Halifax 1998, viii).[18]

The Bodhisattva path is demanding, in terms of intellectual understanding, constant practice, lived realization, and the exercise of compassion. In Chan traditions, however, it is often discussed as the most reasonable response to a deep understanding of the identification between co-dependent origination and emptiness—if I am empty of a permanent, enduring self, but full of all other things, then the suffering of others is my suffering, and my suffering is theirs. Compassion toward any and all suffering is then the most logical and best response, albeit a difficult one that can take many lifetimes. Contemporary Chan Master Sheng Yen writes,

> Bodhisattvas are beings who have vowed to help others find the Buddhist path without concern for their own personal benefit. Chan practitioners and other followers of the bodhisattva path should strive to cultivate such a selfless attitude. . . . Chan practice helps us to lessen self-centeredness in all its guises: greed, attachment, anger, arrogance, escapism, expectation, and so forth. (Yen 2001, 15–16)

One of the things many westerners know about Buddhism (and especially about Zen, the Japanese form of Chan Buddhism) is that it involves meditation. "In the Chan practice of sitting meditation we cultivate a combination of patience, endurance, and tolerance" (Jun 2013, 33). Many Chan texts discuss the practice of "just sitting" as one of the most difficult—and important—things necessary for cultivation. Often our minds are running a constant inner dialogue, hopping from one thing to the next without leaving time or space for self-awareness and stillness. "In Chan, wisdom is coming back to the present moment. It is in the present moment that we see, smell, taste, feel, and think clearly. . . . Wisdom is experiential. In Chan, we say it comes from returning again and again to the present moment" (Jun 2013, 30–31).

In terms of social media engagement, there are some ways in which participation with social media platforms might be seen to aid the path to becoming a bodhisattva. First, there are many large Buddhist communities (*sangha*) around the world and online, and someone who lives in a predominantly non-Buddhist place can use social media to connect with a larger Buddhist community. This means that those interested in the teachings of the Buddha can support and teach one another across physical boundaries. Examples of this include Tibetan Buddhist communities now scattered across the globe that can connect with one another, multinational Buddhist communities online, and online courses in meditation from different Buddhist traditions. These online communities can serve as ways of working on the Four Proper Exertions: helping others to avoid non-virtuous acts not yet performed, persuading others to cease performing non-virtuous acts, encouraging others to engage in wholesome acts not yet performed, and urging others to nurture and expand wholesome acts already performed (Yen 2001, 18–19).

Second, one key Mahayana teaching is co-dependent origination, or the interconnectedness of all events and phenomena. Social media can and does draw attention to the ways in which global interdependence creates and maintains systems of oppression for which we are all responsible. Bodhisattvas are not just concerned with local suffering, but with the suffering of all sentient beings, and they recognize that our interconnectedness entails a strong sense of ethical responsibility even to situations that are distant. In thinking about what Avalokiteshvara (Guanyin) might say to a prostitute in Manila, Thich Nhat Hanh writes, "he would tell her to look deeply at herself and at the whole situation, and see that she is like this because other people are like that. . . . No one among us has clean hands. No one of us can claim that it is not our responsibility" (Hanh 1988, 33). Social media potentially highlight the connections between us in ways that encourage compassionate responses to suffering.

Social media also offers a way of teaching and sharing the *dharma* in short bursts that may be beneficial to students; the Dalai Lama has a Twitter account. Many Mahayana traditions embrace the practice of *upaya*, or expedient means: "the creative devices employed by bodhisattvas in carrying out their vow to liberate all sentient beings. Great bodhisattvas possessed such profound skill in means that there were no situations in which they could not do the buddha-world of awakening" (Hershock 2004, 63). Like many other expedient means, social media might have certain problems, but may also be a valuable site of awakening.

However, there are many ways in which social media engagement might be seen as at best a distraction from the kinds of practices needed for living well, and at worst an active hindrance. One of the primary causes of suffering is identified as ignorance of no-self (*anatman*); from a Buddhist perspective most people are ruled to some degree by the fiction that their self is permanent, unchanging, and essential. However, Buddhists argue that there is no self. So many Buddhist practices are designed to rehabituate students out of self-oriented motivations, thoughts, and actions. One of the real dangers of social media usage is that it can serve as a bastion to the fiction of the self—how many likes did *my* post receive? How many followers do *I* have? What's *my* opinion on this issue? Social media tends to reinforce problematic notions of the self. It also has a tendency to become a sea of inanity, where one's time and attention are submerged in the bombardment of new information, ideas, pictures, blogs, memes, posts—not exactly the stillness and awareness Chan/Buddhist practice strives to develop. With all of that demanding constant attention, there is little time or energy left for focusing on quieting the mind, attending to the fiction of the self, and cultivating compassion toward others. When Huineng, the sixth Chan Patriarch, said that "wisdom is meditation and meditation is wisdom," it's doubtful he could have imagined the increasingly busy and fast-paced world in which we live today, where platforms like Twitter offer a space for disposable thoughts. The advice, however, remains the same: slow down and pay attention. "Quieting the mind is only one facet of the practice because at the core of the [Heart] sutra's teachings are both wisdom and compassion. In fact, one leads to the other. Any insight derived from meditation is incomplete unless imbued and tempered with compassion. We only fully realize the Dharma when we act with both wisdom and compassion" (Yen 2001, 13). That is, the issue is not simply that social media is fast-paced and/or distracting, but that the point of quieting one's mind is to be able to cultivate wisdom and compassion, which are difficult without a quiet mind.

It is not just our ignorance of no-self, but also our attachment to the idea of a self, that brings us suffering. Living well from a Buddhist perspective requires consistent practices of awareness and non-attachment. "From the perspective of Chan, everything is spiritual practice, not only sitting on a meditation cushion. Practice is the moment you wake up until the moment you sleep, every single moment. . . . There is a Buddhist word for this in English: mindfulness" (Jun 2013, 60). By bringing mindfulness into every moment and every action, one can rehabituate oneself out of destructive patterns of thought and behavior: "Every step is a mindful step. Every moment is a mindful moment. Every breath is a mindful breath. If you practice the mindfulness of breath, and yet your kitchen is a mess and your bed is unmade, that is a little bit weird" (Jun 2013, 62). Likewise, if you want to be mindful then spending a large chunk of time losing yourself online in social media may not be conducive to the goal.

Furthermore, the path toward becoming a Bodhisattva is also inextricably tied up with *ahimsa*, non-violence, and compassion. In as much as social media has a tendency to proliferate violent responses to posts, like rape/death threats, bullying, and abusive language, it is not a place for developing compassion for others and oneself, and as such perhaps may be dangerous for the path toward Bodhisattva-hood. Non-violence is not only something to be practiced physically, but also in one's mind and in one's language.

Buddhists are especially concerned with the connections between intention, thought, and action, and as such some contemporary Buddhists have put together guidelines for *mindful* social media usage. Blogger Lori Deschene (2011) compiled ten pieces of advice for Buddhist use of social media: 1. Know your intentions; 2. Be your authentic self; 3. If you propose to tweet, always ask yourself: Is it true? Is it necessary? Is it kind?; 4.

Offer random tweets of kindness; 5. Experience now, share later; 6. Be active, not reactive; 7. Respond with your full attention; 8. Use mobile social media sparingly; 9. Practice letting go; and 10. Enjoy social media. Her advice here is permeated with concerns for the dangers of social media overuse: selfishness, partial attention, attachment, and a lack of compassion toward others. However, one could use social media, from a Buddhist perspective, in ways that are mindful, attentive, and compassionate.

What about non-Chan Buddhists? Other Buddhist traditions may have different kinds of concerns with social media usage. For example, Vajrayana Buddhists engage in a variety of esoteric practices, and so are not supposed to share or discuss their practices with non-initiates; they have explicit instructions for what they can and cannot share with others. Tibetan Buddhist teacher Dzongsar Khyentse Rinpoche issues a series of "Social Media Guidelines" for Vajrayana students, including cautioning students not to share their experiences in practice, not to share whatever attainments or wisdom they think they might have, and to be especially mindful of their motivations for posting/sharing online (2013).

Pure Land Buddhism, one of the most popular forms of Buddhism in East Asia, focuses heavily on the figure of Amida Buddha (who was previously a Bodhisattva). One of the most common practices in Pure Land Buddhism is the sincere recitation of the name of Amida Buddha (*Namo Amituo Fo*), in hopes of receiving Amida's grace to be reborn in the Pure Land. What might be the status of this recitation on social media? Does "liking" a recitation have the same force as reciting it? These are some issues and questions that arise in other Buddhist traditions.

THEY CAN'T GET ON FACEBOOK AND OTHER CONCERNS ABOUT CHINESE INTERNET ACCESS

As the staggering numbers of Chinese social media users might suggest, there are a variety of social media platforms available in China. In fact, of the top twelve social media sites in the world, four are Chinese (Heggenstuen 2013). Top social media sites in China include Sina Weibo, Renren, Tencent Weibo, Qzone, Weixin, Pengyou, Kaixin, Douban, Diandian, Wechat, and Youku (Simcott 2014). Many of these sites are roughly analogous to Facebook, Twitter, Myspace, Tumblr, AIM Instant Messenger, and YouTube. Although many of these sites have users in the hundreds of millions, the Great Firewall is one of the only things many westerners have heard about the internet in China. The Chinese government maintains an active censorship program (The Golden Shield, or "The Great Firewall") that shuts down or prevents access to a variety of websites deemed to contain or promote "superstitious, pornographic, violence-related, gambling and other harmful information" (Xinhua 2010). Well-known western sites such as Google, Wikipedia, Voice of America, and BBC are generally inaccessible in China, and sites that cover sensitive topics such as the Tiananmen Square incident, Taiwan, Tibetan independence, freedom of speech, and the new religious movement Falun Gong are often shut down or difficult to access. Blocked sites also often include famous social media platforms like Facebook, YouTube, and Twitter.[19] However, within China there are a variety of well-known ways around government censorship. For instance, successful searches related to Tiananmen Square often use homophonic plays on the date of the incident, June 4 (that is, 6/4). Virtual Private Networks (VPNs) are also a common way around internal Chinese firewalls, and are relatively easy to purchase and use within China, although censors do catch on and shut down some. Many Chinese citizens maintain active Facebook profiles by using something as simple as a VPN. Motivated people can access external sites with some difficulty.

In addition to external censorship, however, the Great Firewall is perhaps more interestingly able to engage in highly agile internal censorship. Scientists at Carnegie Mellon University in Pittsburgh recently conducted a study of soft censorship of Chinese social media. Study authors David Bamman, Brendan O'Connor, and Noah Smith did a statistical analysis of 56 million messages from Sina Weibo (the Chinese equivalent to Twitter), and 11 million Chinese language messages from Twitter, looking at the active deletion of messages published by individuals. What they found was a set of politically sensitive terms that led, in their words, "to anomalously higher rates of deletion. We also note that the rate of message deletion is not uniform throughout the country, with messages originating in the outlying provinces of Tibet and Qinghai exhibiting much higher deletion rates than those from eastern areas like Beijing" (2012, n.p.) The study found that internal Chinese censorship is not a centralized, black-or-white affair. Some search terms were censored in some areas while not in others, and not all obviously politically sensitive terms (for example, Ai Weiwei, Falun Gong) were blocked or removed from every instance of use. Internal censorship tends to focus more on local events, such as the Wenzhou train crash and the calls for resignation spurred by the crash (Jiang 2011). The authors also found that not all censorship was political in nature: they recorded one incident where censors deleted a strain of microblog entries spreading a false rumor that iodized salt would protect people from radiation.

In addition to government sponsored censorship, however, Chinese social media sites also self-censor in a way that is not common in western countries. Sina Weibo employs more than seven hundred people as censors, in addition to software that checks for politically sensitive key words (Ramzy 2011). Many Chinese people have also found that the opportunities for discussion offered by this Twitter-like platform can be limited, as others do not hesitate to publicly shame users who post on certain topics, or are overtly critical of local or national figures. Some-times this has led to real conversations about corruption and occasionally even resignations, but often it simply results in the original blogger re-treating from the controversy.

Discussions outside of China about Chinese social media invariably address ethical concerns surrounding censorship. One way to situate these discussions, however, is as an example of a much larger and very complex discussion about human rights, where the free access to infor-mation is often assumed to be a fundamental, first-generation right.[20] Documents such as the Bangkok Declaration of Human Rights (1993) and the ASEAN Human Rights Declaration (2012) affirm the importance of human rights while also opening space for culturally diverse expressions of rights, among other things. These documents grew out of the recogni-tion that the very idea of "human rights" is historically and culturally situated in a primarily western tradition of liberal democracies, where concepts like autonomy and self-sufficiency are taken as unquestionably good assumptions. Because some non-western traditions, such as those found in China, do not embrace certain ideals foundational to previous understandings of human rights (and because of histories of western imperialism and colonialism), open dialogue about the very real prob-lems of human rights abuses was difficult. New languaging about cultu-ral and economic plurality, as well as recognition of different state prior-ities in terms of first-, second-, and third-generation rights, has made for more fruitful contemporary discussions.[21] China has consistently main-tained that the state seeks to address second generation rights such as right to education and right to livelihood as necessary to pursue first generation rights like individual liberties without a loss of social order. In a nation of more than one billion people, social order is an understand-able priority. Chinese dynasties stretching back two thousand years have prioritized stability over liberty, and one of the functions of the govern-ment has been moral guidance. The ideal of the sage king, whose person-al character is so moral that he can transform the country, stretches back to early Confucian philosophy and is still active in many ways today. That China today maintains its Golden Shield ostensibly to prevent the dissemination of social ills like pornography is seen by many as a moral duty of the government. This is not to say that they are actually success-ful, or should be. But there does need to be real discussion, not just an assumption that first-generation rights are unquestionably most impor-tant, and this real discussion requires an engagement with China's intel-lectual traditions on their own terms.

CONCLUSION

China and Chinese philosophical traditions have much to offer contemporary discussions on the ethics of social media. Although none of the traditions covered in this essay offer concrete yay/nay arguments concerning social media, the unique perspectives offered by these traditions add to the set of resources for thinking through social media and living well in a global context. Perspectives from these traditions do, however, agree at least that social media is generally a second-best way of interacting with others, and that engaging in social media while attempting to live a certain kind of life comes with specific cautions. Although the ethical exemplar may perhaps gain some benefits from social media use, the dangers for the unskilled are substantial. In addition, when examining issues of ethics and social media, we would be remiss not to consider the actual situation of social media in China, and should try to think through Chinese perspectives on social media without uncritically importing western assumptions into the discourse.

NOTES

1. With the exception of discussions of the Arab Spring, which focus on the role of social media in political change.
2. Although in English we use the term "Confucianism," this is based on the Latinized version of the name of Kongfuzi, "Confucius," and is in fact not how the tradition is identified in Chinese. Kongzi was one of many *Ru*, or ritual masters, who taught during the Spring and Autumn and Warring States period, and the tradition in Chinese is known as the Ru Lineage (*Rujia*).
3. In addition to the *Analects*, see for example the *Daxue (The Great Learning)*, which describes the project of personal cultivation as located along a continuum of cultivation projects moving from the personal to the familial, social, political, and cosmic, and back again.
4. Although there are some key examples of Confucian literati engaging in political critique while knowing that it meant their death.
5. "Louis C. K. Hates Cell Phones." Video Interview from *The Conan Show*, September 20, 2013. Retrieved July 8, 2014 from teamcoco.com/video/louis-ck-springsteen-cell-phone.
6. During and after the Han Dynasty, a variety of figures known as the Celestial Masters become increasingly important.
7. In their introduction to the *Daodejing*, Roger Ames and David Hall describe these dispositions in terms of the *wu*-forms: *wu-wei* (non-coercive action), *wu-zhi* (non-principled knowing), *wu-yu* (objectless desire).
8. Many western thinkers find the common distinction between *Daojia* (philosophical Daoism) and *Daojiao* (Religious Daoism) to be helpful; however, this distinction is not as rigid or as helpful as many scholars would suggest.
9. For this passage, see *Zhuangzi*, Chapter 5. In traditional Chinese culture physical deformity of any kind was often associated with moral depravity, low-class standing, or criminality. So for Confucius to want Wang Tai, with his foot probably chopped off due to theft, as a teacher, is a radical reversal of social conventions of the time.
10. For this passage, see *Zhuangzi*, Chapter 6.

11. There may be some possible counterexamples to this such as online art communities. However, generally speaking for Daoists the physicality and embodied action of the art practice is especially important.

12. My thanks to Dr. Ethan Mills for passing along this joke.

13. Rather than a single monolithic tradition, Buddhism is better described as Buddhisms, as there are many diverse traditions that fall under the loose heading of Buddhism. The term "Buddhism" itself is a product of western religious construction: for more on this see *The Invention of World Religion* by Tomoko Masuzawa.

14. For more on this, see Hershock, *Chan Buddhism*, 13.

15. The question of whether or not to include Tibetan Buddhism as a school of Chinese Buddhism is immersed in a long and complicated political situation. Currently the PRC includes Tibetan Buddhism as a school of Chinese Buddhism.

16. In the contemporary world, Mahayana Buddhism is most associated with East Asia, Theravada with South East Asia, and Vajrayana with Tibetan Buddhism and Shingon Buddhism in Japan.

17. For more on the history and nature of Chan Buddhism, see also Hershock 2004.

18. Although not Chinese, the Buddhism that Thich Nhat Hanh teaches is from the Vietnamese Zen school, which has its roots in Chinese Chan Buddhism.

19. Recently China has unblocked Facebook and Twitter in some parts of Shanghai.

20. Article 8 of the Bangkok Declaration came to represent the high watermark of cultural relativism: "while human rights are universal in nature, they must be considered in the context of a dynamic and evolving process of international norm-setting, bearing in mind the significance of national and regional particularities and various historical, cultural and religious backgrounds."

21. For more on this, see Ames 1997 "Continuing the Conversation on Chinese Human Rights"; Donnelly 1997 "Conversing with Straw Men While Ignoring Dictators"; Steve Angle 2002 *Human Rights and Chinese Thought: A Cross-Cultural Inquiry* and *The Chinese Human Rights Reader: Documents and Commentaries 1900–2000.*

REFERENCES

Bamman, D., O'Connor, B., and N. Smith. (2012). "Censorship and Deletion Practices in Chinese Social Media." *First Monday* 17, 3–5.

Bockover, M. (2003). "Confucian Values and the Internet: A Potential Conflict." *Journal of Chinese Philosophy* 30, 2.

Chiu, C., Ip, C., and A. Silverman. (2012, April). "Understanding Social Media in China." Retrieved July 7, 2014 from www.mckinsey.com/insights/marketing_sales/understanding_social_media_in_china.

Dao De Jing: A Philosophical Translation (2003). Trans. R. T. Ames and D. L. Hall. New York: Ballantine Books.

Deschene, L. (2011, Spring). "Ten Mindful Ways to Use Social Media." Retrieved July 7, 2014 from www.tricycle.com/feature/ten-mindful-ways-use-social-media.

Granet, M. (1934). *Le Pensee Chinoise.* Paris: Editions Albin Michel.

Halifax, J. (1998). "The Road is Your Footsteps." In T. H. Hahn, *For a Future to be Possible.* Berkeley: Parallax Press, vi–xi.

Hanh, T. N. (1988). *The Heart of Understanding: Commentary on the Prajnaparamita Heart Sutra.* Berkeley: Parallax Press.

Heggenstuen, J. (2013, November 5). "Confused By China's Social Networks? Here's A Simple Infographic Showing Their US-Based Equivalents." Retrieved July 7, 2014 from www.businessinsider.com/a-quick-guide-to-chinas-social-networks-2013-10#ixzz36oa3YzNn.

Hershock, P. (2004). *Chan Buddhism.* Honolulu: University of Hawaii Press.

Jiang, S. (2011, July 26). "Chinese Netizens Outraged over Response to Fatal Bullet Train Crash." Retrieved July 7, 2014 from www.cnn.com/2011/WORLD/asiapcf/07/25/china.train.accident.outrage/.

Jun, G. (2013). *Essential Chan Buddhism: The Character and Spirit of Chinese Zen*. New York: Monkfish Book Publishing.

"Louis C.K. Hates Cell Phones." Video Interview from *The Conan Show*, September 20, 2013. Retrieved July 8, 2014 from teamcoco.com/video/louis-ck-springsteen-cell-phone.

Mengzi (2008). 1A7. *Mengzi: With Selections from Traditional Commentaries*, translated by Bryan W. Van Norden. Indianapolis: Hackett Publishing.

Millward, S. (2013, March13). "Check Out the Numbers on China's Top 10 Social Media Sites." Retrieved July 7, 2014 from www.techinasia.com/2013-china-top-10-social-sites-infographic/.

Ramzy, A. (2011, February 17). "Wired Up." Retrieved July 7, 2014 from content.time.com/time/magazine/article/0,9171,2048171-1,00.html.

Rinpoche, D. K. (2013, January 17). "Social Media Guidelines for So-Called Vajrayana Students." Retrieved July 7, 2014 from shambhalasun.com/sunspace/?p=31004.

Simcott, R. (2014, February 27). "Social Media Fast Facts: China." Retrieved July 7, 2014 from socialmediatoday.com/richard-simcott/2213841/social-media-fast-facts-china.

The Analects of Confucius: A Philosophical Translation. (1998). Trans. R. T. Ames and H. Rosemont Jr. New York: Ballantine Books.

Wong, P. (2013) "Confucian Social Media: An Oxymoron?" *Dao: A Journal of Comparative Philosophy* 12, 283–296.

Xinhua News Agency (2010). "China and the Internet." *International Debates* 8, 4.

Yen, S. (2001). *There Is No Suffering: A Commentary on the Heart Sutra*. New York: Dharma Drum Publications.

Index

About the Contributors

Alan B. Albarran is a professor and chair of the Department of Radio, Television and Film at the University of North Texas. The author of fifteen books, his research and teaching interests revolve around the management and economics of the media industries.

Berrin A. Beasley is associate professor of communication at the University of North Florida.

Paul Bloomfield is professor of philosophy at the University of Connecticut (Storrs). He is the author of *The Virtues of Happiness*, as well as *Moral Reality*, and the editor of *Morality and Self-Interest*.

Frederick R. "Randy" Carlson is the Poynter Jamison Scholar in media ethics and press policy at the University of South Florida, St. Petersburg. His research interests are the privacy, business, and ethics issues that appear at the intersection of journalism and cyberspace. He has twenty-two years of experience as a systems engineer in large-scale computer and communication network projects.

Deni Elliott holds the Eleanor Poynter Jamison Chair in media ethics and press policy at the University of South Florida, St. Petersburg. She is chair of the Department of Journalism and Media Studies and is Campus Ombudsman. Her newest book, *Ethics for a Digital Era*, will be published by Wiley-Blackwell in 2015.

Ken Gilroy is a patent-winning creative executive who develops content that allows consumers to establish authentic connections across multiple digital and physical platforms. Over the course of his career, he's done everything from help shape the Care Bears brand as a licensed property at retail to leading creative studios in Paris focused on developing mobile content. He currently resides in northeast Ohio, and focuses his talents on solving puzzles around digital media and new product development.

Mitchell R. Haney is associate professor of philosophy and co-director of the Florida Blue Center for Ethics at the University of North Florida.

Sarah Mattice is an assistant professor in the Department of Philosophy and Religious Studies at the University of North Florida. She specializes in comparative philosophy, East Asian philosophy, and aesthetics.

Katherine Brittain Richardson is professor of communication at Berry College, Rome, Georgia, where she has served as provost since 2013. She holds a BA in communication and religion/philosophy from Shorter College and an MA in journalism and a PhD in mass communication from the Grady College of Journalism and Mass Communication at The University of Georgia. She is coauthor of *Media Ethics Cases and Moral Reasoning* and *Applied Public Relations: Cases in Stakeholder Management.*

Joseph Ulatowski is visiting assistant professor of philosophy at the University of Texas at El Paso. His philosophical work on social media has been featured in interviews with Wyoming Public Television and with the nationally syndicated internet radio program *The Social Network Show*.

Pamela A. Zeiser is associate professor of political science at the University of North Florida. Her research interests include global health politics, U.S. foreign policy, political science pedagogy, and interdisciplinary studies.